chicken

THE NEW CLASSICS

chicken

THE NEW CLASSICS

Marcus Bean

NOURISH

EAT WELL, LIVE WELL

DEDICATION
For Jenny, Ella and Ava. And for all the chickens out there being used in rubbish recipes – it's time to cook you properly!

Chicken
Marcus Bean

This edition first published in the UK and Ireland in 2015 by
Nourish, an imprint of Watkins Media Limited
19 Cecil Court
London WC2N 4EZ

enquiries@nourishbooks.com

Publisher: Grace Cheetham
Project Editor: Rebecca Woods
Editor: Wendy Hobson
Designer: Manisha Patel
Production: Uzma Taj
Commissioned photography: Martin Poole, except for
    page 7, Victoria Macken
Food Stylist: Aya Nishimura
Prop Stylist: Wei Tang

A CIP record for this book is available from the British Library

ISBN: 978-1-84899-160-6

10 9 8 7 6 5 4 3 2

Typeset in Filosofia
Colour reproduction by PDQ, UK
Printed in China

Publisher's note
While every care has been taken in compiling the recipes for
this book, Watkins Media Limited, or any other persons who
have been involved in working on this publication, cannot
accept responsibility for any errors or omissions, inadvertent
or not, that may be found in the recipes or text, nor for any
problems that may arise as a result of preparing one of these
recipes. If you are pregnant or breastfeeding or have any
special dietary requirements or medical conditions, it is
advisable to consult a medical professional before following
any of the recipes contained in this book. Ill or elderly people,
babies, young children and women who are pregnant or
breastfeeding should avoid recipes containing raw meat or
fish or uncooked eggs.

Notes on the recipes
Unless otherwise stated:
· Use free-range eggs and poultry
· Use medium eggs, fruit and vegetables
· Use fresh ingredients, including herbs and chillies
· Do not mix metric and imperial measurements
· 1 tsp = 5ml 1 tbsp = 15ml 1 cup = 250ml

nourishbooks.com

contents

introduction

Always one of my favourite ingredients, chicken is succulent, flavoursome, versatile, inexpensive and healthy. It's very popular in our house as my wife, Jenny, hasn't eaten red meat since she was a child, so I've cooked more chicken than most, but we never get fed up with it – why should we? Few foods blend as well with such a range of different ingredients and flavourings, so there's always something different to try. In fact, I can't think of anything that couldn't be successfully paired with chicken to make a delicious meal – from delicate to robust foods, from subtle, creamy sauces to hot fiery curries, fruit or vegetables, fish or cheese, herbs, spices or nuts, rices, pulses or pasta. Plus, as there are mouth-watering chicken dishes in every cuisine around the world – from curries to oriental stir-fries or chicken and chips – the sky's the limit.

For a modern and health-conscious diet, too, chicken ticks all the boxes as it is both low in fat and a great source of protein. A 100g/3½oz serving of baked chicken breast contains 4g of fat and 31g of protein, compared with 10g of fat and 27g of protein for the same portion of grilled lean steak. This makes it a sensible and nutritious part of a healthy balanced diet, and great for those who are trying to slim down a little, too – cooked in the right way, of course.

Chicken is also fantastically versatile. It can be cooked by almost any cooking method – slowly for a succulent casserole, or quickly with a crisp, pan-fried skin. The various cuts lend themselves to every different style of cooking, giving us so many choices that we can keep the interest going in our meals – even if we were to eat chicken every day.

As well as its versatility, in these budget-conscious times, chicken scores highly as an inexpensive meat. And the fact that nothing is wasted – even the carcase makes wonderful soup or stock – is an added bonus. It's hard to think of a better set of credentials for any ingredient to be chosen as the star of a book and I hope you'll enjoy seeing it in the spotlight.

So I am delighted to be able to share some of my favourite chicken recipes with you. In writing this book, I set out to discover as much as I could about chicken and why we love it so much, and I have created recipes that I hope will inspire you to experiment and enjoy this fabulous meat as much as I do. I have set out to give you the best of the classic chicken recipes, experimenting with modern and unexpected twists along the way. But I have also created new recipes, exploring great flavour combinations that I hope will help you to revolutionize the way you cook with chicken.

THE ICONIC RECIPES

Because of chicken's versatility, cooks around the world have all taken chicken into their kitchens and created some of the most delicious recipes, each one with that perfect balance of ingredients. Some are recognized pairings, others evolved from happy accident, resulting in flavours, textures, colours and cooking methods that make a really classic dish. These dishes have stood the test of time, and some of them are a starting point for my own recipes in this book.

Coq au vin was one of the first dishes I mastered as a chef, and I just had to include a classic version (see page 110) because it is a recipe that still fits perfectly into our modern lifestyle. 'Cockerel with wine' is known by every chef around the world. Based on the classic principles of French cuisine, this slow braise of chicken in red wine with mushrooms, bacon lardons and garlic makes a rich and warming dish. Created in the early twentieth century, its popularity was assured by the TV chef Julia Child, who featured the dish on her TV show and in the breakthrough 1961 cookbook, *Mastering the Art of French Cooking*, which she co-wrote with S. Beck and L. Bertholle.

Another recipe that I just had to include was a version of Caesar salad. In the 1920s, the Italian immigrant restaurateur, Caesar Cardini, was running a successful business in the USA and Mexico. The story goes that after a rush in one of his restaurants, he would take all the ingredients he had left in the kitchen table-side and create a salad for the customer. Caesar salad emerged from that imaginative blending of ingredients: Romaine lettuce, croûtons, Parmesan cheese, lemon juice, olive oil, egg, Worcestershire sauce, garlic and black pepper. Cooks have continued to experiment, adapt and tweak it in an infinite number of ways, including adding chicken to the recipe, and I have carried on that tradition. My modern version takes each element individually so they can shine in their own right. I hope you will enjoy my Deconstructed Crispy Pancetta & Charred Lettuce Caesar Salad with Anchovy Straws (see page 141).

I've always loved chicken Kiev – a dish of battered chicken wrapped around cold garlic butter, breadcrumbed and fried to a golden and crispy finish. Traditionally considered Ukrainian in origin – hardly surprising since Kiev is the capital of Ukraine – the Russian food historian William Pokhlebkin insists that it was invented in the Moscow Merchants' Club in the early twentieth century, and was later renamed chicken Kiev when it was marketed for restaurants in Europe. I have taken it to another continent in my Asian-Style Chicken Kiev (see page 188) to give it a whole new dimension.

Another recent classic, fajitas – or 'little meat' – became popular in the 1990s, spreading around the world from its home in Mexican and American restaurants with its characteristic sizzle. So often, we reach for the ready-made options when we enjoy this dish with family and friends, but I hope my Chicken Fajitas & Homemade Smoked Paprika Wraps (see page 42) will encourage you to make it all from scratch. It's easier than you'd think.

Back home in the UK, I had to include the true British classic, roast chicken. I fondly remember growing up in the pub and how we used to gather on Sunday for a family meal of roast chicken, often with as many as eight extra guests – usually friends of mine invited at the last minute. Even though the popularity of the traditional Sunday roast is waning as our lifestyles change, roast chicken still appears regularly on lunch and dinner tables, on Sundays or any day of the week, accompanied by roast potatoes, vegetables and gravy (although serving Yorkshire pudding remains contentious, many people insisting that it only goes with beef). When I roast chicken, I always know it is going to be tender and succulent because I soak it in brine before cooking. Try Lemon Verbena & Thyme-Roasted Chicken (see page 132) and you'll enjoy succulent herb-scented meat.

CHICKEN BREEDS
So let's take a step back to find out a little about these valuable birds. Around 5,000 years ago in Asia, the red jungle fowl gradually gave rise to the modern chicken, which is now one of the most common and widespread domestic animals in the world. Estimates suggest that the worldwide chicken population is well over 24 billion (although I have no idea who counts them all!). That means there are more chickens in the world than any other species of bird. More than 50 billion chickens are reared annually as a source of food, and we eat both their meat and their eggs. In the UK alone, we eat more than 29 million eggs every day, so it's a good thing that some breeds of hen can produce over 300 eggs per year, the record being a fairly staggering 371.

There are hundreds of different breeds of chicken around the world, and even more cross-breeds, each with its own characteristics defined in terms of its place of origin, size, plumage and colour. Generally speaking, each breed is better for producing either eggs or meat, although some breeds are considered dual purpose. Farmers or individuals therefore have plenty of choice to select the breed that will give them the best results, depending on their circumstances and whether they want prolific egg-layers or particular flavours of meat.

Among the most valued egg-layers are the Rhode Island Red, the New Hampshire Red and the Australorp. These breeds all have the added advantage that they are good foragers and don't fly well, making it easier to keep them safely in a farmyard or garden. The Australorp is particularly noted for its docile temperament, another reason why it is a good hen for beginners.

One of the most notable breeds for meat is the French Poulet de Bresse, which produces such a high-quality product that it is sought after by chefs all over the world, while the French chefs endeavour to use most of it at home. Popular dual-purpose birds include the Orpington, the Plymouth Rock, a particularly good choice for those in colder areas, and the Sussex.

And that's just the hens. There are also the cockerels – the males that are less than a year old – and the cocks, or roosters as they call them in the US. The meat from a cock chicken tends to be slightly tougher but is great for stocks, broths and slow-cooked casseroles, as are boiling fowl, which are also over one year old. A poussin, or spring chicken, is a smaller bird, ideal for individual servings.

As I write, we have three cockerels that roam around weeding the flower beds for us. We keep our hens at my mother-in-law's as she tends all the chickens to supply us with eggs and meat. We use them for our bed and breakfast, our cookery school and, of course, for our breakfast every day. Our plan is to keep more hens at home very soon.

INTENSIVE FARMING & ORGANIC FARMING
Until the middle of the twentieth century, chicken was regarded as a luxury and graced the tables only on special occasions. It was the advent of intensive rearing methods that changed its status, making chicken both plentiful and inexpensive, and it is now the most commonly eaten meat around the world.

Of course, that came with disadvantages – not least for the chickens – including overcrowding, poor health and being kept constantly caged. Non-free-range birds feed on grain coated with antibiotics to improve their resistance to disease, while living in cramped conditions. The meat is often bland and tasteless, and is sometimes pumped with water to make it more tender

Adverse reaction to intensive poultry farming has led to the resurgence of the old ways, and many people – including me – seek out both eggs and meat from organic and free-range chickens because the way the chicken is raised affects

both the quality of the meat and also the quality of the eggs – quite apart from any ethical considerations. The only difference between a free-range and a free-range organic bird is that the organic birds are not routinely fed antibiotics or artificial supplements to maintain their general health.

Both free-range and organic birds are fed corn mix and are allowed to roam outside in the daytime in the fields or open spaces and forage for feed such as insects, worms, clover, herbs or flowers. This means they have a more natural and varied diet, which adds both flavour to the meat and also improves the quality, colour and flavour of the eggs.

The relaxed environment also allows them to develop in their own time, being given about 14 weeks to mature, while intensively farmed chickens are slaughtered at six weeks. As the free-range birds can roam the farmyard, the chickens build stronger muscles in both the legs and breast, giving the meat a firmer texture as well as more intense flavour. That is why my favourite way to cook chicken legs is to cook them slowly and gently in oil to make a confit, or in a casserole to break down the muscle until it is so tender it simply falls off the bone.

RAISING CHICKENS AT HOME
Many people raise their own hens, which is not difficult in an ordinary garden as all you need is a small amount of land and enough room for a cage and an open-air run. Although they certainly can't fly very high or very far, you must not forget that domestic chickens are not completely flightless, although their skills in this department do vary considerably. Some breeds, especially the lighter birds, can fly short distances, such as over fences or into trees (where they would naturally roost), so you can make it easier if you choose breeds that are poor flyers.

Incidentally, egg-laying hens do not need males to produce eggs, only to fertilize them, so an all-female flock will still produce eggs for you, even though the eggs will all be infertile.

Whatever you choose, I'm sure you'll get as much enjoyment out of keeping chickens as we do. Apart from the eggs and meat, they are such lovely creatures to have around. I know several people who have been worn down by their family's enthusiasm and only reluctantly agreed to keep chickens but who have since become their strongest advocate. I love going out in the morning and bringing back a basket of the freshest of eggs for our breakfast, cracking them into a pan to reveal their bright yolks, then enjoying the rich, creamy flavour.

buying chicken

When it comes to buying chicken, my preference is for a good free-range, preferably organic, bird because, as we have seen, this gives a superior flavour and texture to both the eggs and the meat. My favourite place to buy a chicken would always be direct from a farm shop, as you can see how the chickens are reared and talk to the people who tend them. You get a real sense of where your food is coming from and I try and do this with all the meat and vegetables I buy. It also helps to inspire me to create new recipe ideas. You may have a local butcher or farm shop near you, but many supermarkets also stock superior-quality products. In addition, the internet now gives you access to great-quality free-range and organic chicken direct from the farms and delivered to your door, so no one needs to miss out on great-quality meat.

A good supplier will keep their meat in a chill cabinet at the correct temperature, well wrapped and with an appropriate use-by date. If it has already been frozen, that should be indicated as you should not refreeze chicken. The birds should be plump and firm, with white, unbroken skin, or yellow for a corn-fed chicken. If you have sensibly left your meat shopping until last, the meat will spend the shortest amount of time out of the fridge.

CUTS OF CHICKEN
A good supplier will offer whole birds, which usually work out cheaper, or a variety of cuts. If you buy from a butcher, you can buy a whole chicken and ask for it to be prepared in any way you want so you have one less thing to think about before you start cooking. Most butchers will bone your chicken thighs to save you time, and even give you free carcasses for stock. Just ask! They normally give them to restaurants or dispose of them. Once you've made the stock you can freeze it down in batches to keep until you need it (see page 197).

Whole
An average chicken weighs about 1.4–1.8 kg/3lb 2oz–4lb but larger birds can weigh up to 2.75kg/6lb. The simplest way to cook a whole chicken is to roast it just with a touch of seasoning, but I like to soak it in a herb-infused brine before I cook it to make sure it is extra moist and succulent (see page 17).

Half
A half-chicken has been cut through the centre of the breast with a pair of heavy kitchen scissors or poultry shears, removing the spine in the process. Half-chickens can also be roasted but are great on the barbecue or grill, too, especially when the skin is rubbed with spices.

Supreme

A supreme is the breast with the wing attached and weighs about 200g/7oz. By leaving the wing on, it allows the breast to retain a little more moisture, although the choice of serving chicken supremes is mainly one of presentation as they look good on the plate. Supremes are most often pan-fried, but can otherwise be cooked in the same ways as the breast. One of my favourite recipes for chicken supremes is Crispy-Skinned Chicken with Sweet Potato Purée, Kale & Crispy Leeks (see page 127), a colourful dish with loads of contrasting textures.

Breast

Breasts are white meat with no bone, usually weighing 125–225g/4½–8oz. Great whole or diced for every kind of cooking method, from pan-frying and grilling to poaching, casseroles and stir-fries, they are quick to cook but can tend to dry out if overcooked. Using a digital meat thermometer will help you avoid this. Check the internal temperature when you think the chicken is ready, then remember that the meat can still carry on cooking for a minute or two once you remove it from the heat, so leave it to rest for a few minutes after cooking. If you are frying, cook with the skin on as this also helps to keep the meat moist.

Cuts of chicken
1 Thighs
2 Drumsticks
3 Fillets
4 Breast
5 Supreme
6 Drumette
7 Middle and tip of wings

Wings

Often served as a light meal or snack, the wings offer a good flavour with a mix of light and dark meat. They fry or roast well and are cooked with the skin on. There are three segments to the wings: the drumette is shaped like a small drumstick; the middle, flat segment contains two bones; and the tip is generally discarded as it has little meat on it, although you can put it in with your stock meat.

Leg

The whole leg can be sold as a cut, or divided into the thigh, the upper part, and the drumstick. Both are dark meat, which generally has more a lot more flavour than the breast and is moister in texture. The meat can be fried, roasted, poached or grilled, or it can be slow-cooked in casseroles or stews. The thigh meat particularly loves to be slow cooked until tender and falling apart. Legs can be cooked with or without the skin and can be boned before cooking, either to make them easier to eat, or for stuffing. The drumsticks make great quick snack food.

Giblets

It's a shame that most people tend to throw away the giblets – the little bundle of parts sometimes found inside the cavity of a bird. They usually include the neck, the gizzard (a muscle that grinds up food before it enters the digestive system), the heart and the liver. I like to use the giblets to make a stock, which I add to the pan after I've roasted a chicken to make a fabulous gravy. You could try that yourself, or add them to my Chicken Stock recipe for extra flavour (see page 197), then use that stock to make your gravy.

Liver

The liver is the largest organ of the chicken and is often sold separately. It is generally used in pâtés, parfaits and terrines, or simply pan-fried in butter. The texture is very light and delicate, and it goes really well with rich foods like cream and butter, and also strong flavours like smoked bacon and herbs. Sometimes there's nothing better than a good spread of homemade chicken liver parfait on hot toast with butter. Try my version, Chicken Liver & Sweet Wine Jelly Parfait, for the perfect treat (see page 152).

Carcase

After the removal of the flesh, the bones and remaining attached meat can be used for making soups and stock (see page 197). Your local butcher may well give you some spare carcases – otherwise they normally give them to restaurants or just dispose of them.

STORING CHICKEN

Everyone knows that you have to be careful with chicken and make sure you handle and store it correctly because, if you don't, it can be prone to developing harmful bacteria. Having said that, if you follow a few common-sense rules, you won't have any problems. But because I want you to enjoy your chicken, here's just a quick reminder how to deal with it.

You should always keep raw or cooked chicken in the fridge, which should be at or below 3–5°C/37–41°F. If you are not sure whether your fridge is working efficiently, you can buy – or, better still, borrow – a fridge thermometer. The place for raw meat is at the bottom of the fridge so there is no chance it will drip on other food. Keep any cooked meat separately at the top of the fridge. Both raw and cooked chicken can be stored in the fridge for about four days, but do keep an eye on the use-by date and follow your instinct – if you are not happy that the meat still looks and smells fresh, then don't use it.

Your meat may already be packaged when you buy it, but if not, wrap it in cling film and put it on a plate to catch any inevitable drips. To make sure it is well sealed, I use a vacuum sealer, which removes all the air and seals the chicken in a bag. You can buy small versions that are great for using at home – and you can use them for wrapping all sorts of foods for the fridge or the freezer, so they have loads more uses than just wrapping chicken. Once refrigerated, meat that you have vacuum-packed will stay fresh for twice as long as meat wrapped in cling film or just in a plastic bag, so it is also much more hygienic.

If you want to freeze chicken, I always recommend that you buy the chicken fresh, make sure it is properly wrapped, then label and freeze it yourself. However, if you do buy frozen chicken, make sure you get it back in the freezer as quickly as possible so it does not start to defrost. Freezers should run at below −20°C/−4°F or colder and although you can keep meat frozen for ages, you should use it within three months for the best flavour and texture.

Allow plenty of time to defrost your chicken before you cook it. Remove it from the freezer, place it on a tray in the fridge and leave it to defrost slowly over about 24 hours. Once fully defrosted, cook it within 24 hours. It is possible to cook smaller cuts from frozen but you just need to be aware that it will take at least twice as long to cook as unfrozen chicken, and you must ensure that you cook it through thoroughly, preferably using a digital thermometer to check. Once defrosted, don't refreeze chicken.

preparing chicken

You may want to ask your butcher to prepare your chicken, or simply buy ready-prepared meat, but it is more economical to buy a whole chicken to joint and prepare, so why not have a go. You will find that, with a little practice, it will soon become second nature. It is really important to have at least one good-quality knife in the kitchen. A sharp knife will make a massive difference to your cooking, from chopping to crushing to filleting.

Just the same as with proper storage, remember a few common-sense hygiene rules when you are preparing chicken. There's no need to wash chicken before you cook it. In fact, the nasty microbes or bacteria are destroyed by proper cooking, whereas you are much more likely to spread them around the kitchen if you are trying to wash the bird in the sink. Keep other ingredients out of the way while you get your chicken ready, so there are fewer chances of cross-contamination, especially with raw foods. Don't answer the phone if it rings or rake through the knife drawer. Concentrate on the chicken, then clear up all your working tools, knives and so on. Wash your hands, all your work surfaces and your utensils with antibacterial hand wash or cleaner, then dry them with disposable cloths or kitchen paper.

TRUSSING A BIRD FOR ROASTING

If you like, you can secure a bird neatly with string, using some kitchen twine. Some cooks feel it helps the chicken cook more evenly, others disagree. For normal roasting, it is a matter of choice. However, if you are cooking the chicken on a barbecue, or especially a rotisserie, so it is going to be turned frequently, it is a good idea as it keeps the bird neatly together and makes cooking much easier. You can also truss a bird for brining.

1 Place the bird on its back and fold the tip of the wings in under the bird so they are tucked in snugly.
2 Take a piece of kitchen twine and run it under the legs. Cross the string over, then wrap each end of the string under the opposite leg.
3 Pull the string tight to pull the legs together firmly.
4 Run the strings around the sides of the chicken, making sure it passes over the wings and thighs as you go, to hold them in position.
5 Turn the chicken over and tie the ends of the string together under the base of the neck bone.
6 The trussed chicken is now ready for roasting.

BRINING

Brining is soaking chicken in salted water before roasting or smoking in order to keep the meat moist when it is cooking or smoking. You can brine chicken for any of the recipes in this book.

FOR THE BRINE:
300g/10½oz/heaped 1 cup salt
2 large lemon verbena sprigs
1 carrot, peeled and halved
1 garlic bulb, cut in half horizontally
100ml/3½fl oz/scant ½ cup light soy sauce
2 large thyme sprigs
1 onion, halved

Dissolve the brine ingredients in 6l/1.3 gallons/ 25 cups water. Add the chicken, making sure that it is covered in the brine. Cover and leave in the fridge overnight, or for about 12 hours. Drain well, rinse, then drain again before cooking.

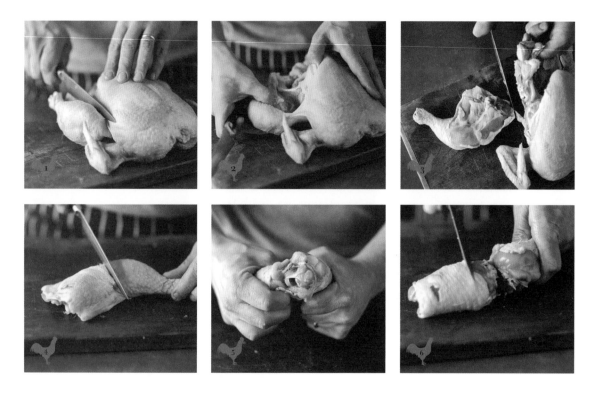

JOINTING A CHICKEN

1 Set the chicken on a secure board and cut off any string. Using a sharp knife, slit the skin between the thigh and the breast and move the leg away from the body so that you can see the joint.

2 Pull the leg fully away from the body and the leg joint will pop out.

3 Run the knife through the joint to separate the leg. Repeat with the other leg. This will give you the two legs, each with the drumstick and the thigh together.

4 To separate the thigh and the drumstick, put the leg on the board and run your finger down the drumstick until you can feel the joint. Slice through the skin at the joint.

5 Hold the leg firmly at either end, then bend the leg in half to break the leg into two at the joint.

6 If you need to, use the knife to finish separating the two pieces by cutting through at the joint.

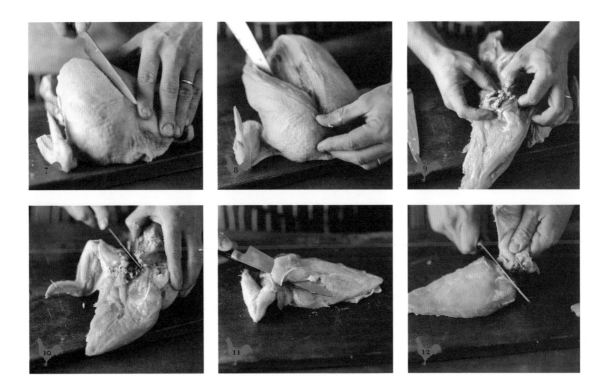

7 Smooth the skin over the breast. Scrape along the wishbone, using a small knife, then slip your fingers under the bone and snap it out in two pieces to make it easier to cut away the breast. To remove the supreme (the breast and wing), slowly run a sharp knife along the breastbone.

8 Gradually run the knife down against the inner bone to allow the breast to come away from the carcase.

9 The chicken breast will still be attached at the bottom by the wing. Slowly pop the wing out of the socket.

10 Run your knife around to release the supreme.

11 The fillets are the small, loose pieces of flesh on the under side of the breast. Simply slice these away with a knife, if required.

12 If you only want the breast, slowly cut round the base of the wing to release and debone the breast. Keep the carcase and trimmings for stock.

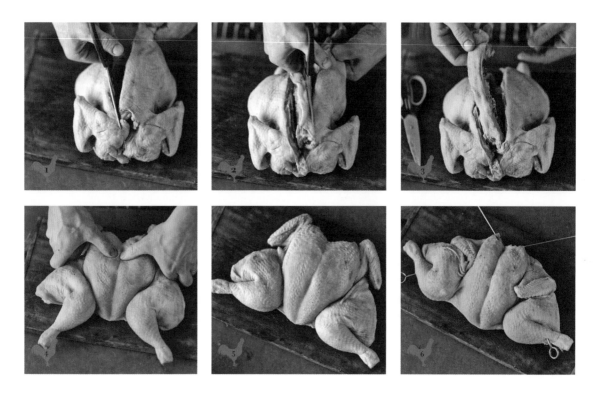

SPATCHCOCKING A BIRD

1 Place the bird on its breast and, using a pair of sharp kitchen shears, cut down along one side of the back bone.

2 Cut down along the other side of the back bone in the same way.

3 Remove the back bone.

4 Turn the chicken over and slowly push down on the breast to flatten the bird.

5 The chicken is now ready for cooking.

6 If you wish, you can insert 2 skewers diagonally through the bird, which will hold the chicken in place and conduct the heat through the thickest part of the chicken, making it cook more quickly and evenly.

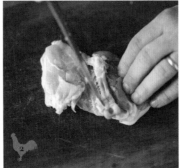
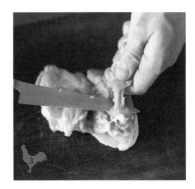

BONING A THIGH

1 Place the thigh on the work surface, then turn it over so that the skin is underneath.
2 Using a sharp knife, cut along the bone to release the flesh.
3 Deepen the cut, running your knife along the bone, then pull the bone away from the thigh, cutting it free as you do so.

TUNNEL BONING A LEG

1 Grasp the leg by the drumstick joint and use a sharp knife to cut around the top of the leg to release all the tendons.
2 Taking the drumstick in one hand and the thigh in the other, bend the leg right back until you hear the joint break and the bones are separated.
3 Grasp the end of the drumstick bone and pull hard to pull the bone all the way through the drumstick and remove it. Remove the thigh bone in the same way, making sure that you remove all of the material around the joint as you do so.

cooking chicken

The trick with cooking chicken is to match the right technique with the right cut. For example, the breast is perfect for quick cooking methods like frying, while the legs really benefit from slow cooking to break down the muscle and allow the meat to become tender and fall off the bone. Whichever method you choose, chicken must always be thoroughly cooked to the right temperature before serving. Test the meat by using a temperature probe to check that it has reached a core temperature of 75°C/167°F, or by pushing a skewer or the tip of a sharp knife into the thickest part to check that the juices run clear, not pink. But avoid piercing the meat until you are pretty sure it is ready, otherwise you will allow the precious juices to drain out. Once cooked, allow the meat just a few minutes to relax and you will find that the meat is much more succulent and tender.

PAN-FRYING

In our busy lives, we often need something that will cook quickly, so pan-fried chicken is a great option. Melt a little butter or oil in a heavy-based frying pan over a medium to high heat and, when it is hot and bubbling, add the chicken. Cook it skin-side down first to give a crisp skin and help to seal in moisture. I like to fry it until it is coloured and sealed, then finish it in a hot oven, but you can simply cook in the pan until the meat is tender.

This method is best for breast meat and imparts a lovely colour and texture to the chicken. You can cook the breasts whole, in which case this is one of the best ways to get a lovely crispy skin, or slice the meat into goujons or strips for stir-frying quickly over a high heat. Halfway between frying and grilling, if you use a chargrill pan to cook chicken, you'll get attractive dark bars across the meat.

GRILLING

Like frying, grilling cooks the meat quickly under a direct heat. Preheat the grill, season the meat and put it on the grill pan. The burst of heat will seal the outside of the meat, retaining the juices inside, then continue to cook until the meat is cooked through, turning as necessary. Because there is no additional oil, this is thought to be a slightly healthier option than frying. You can grill any cut of chicken, just make sure the heat is not too high that it overcooks the outside before the meat is cooked through.

BARBECUE

I love cooking any cuts of chicken on a barbecue, with the extra smoky flavour added to the grilling process. Those with a gas barbecue can add a few smoking chips onto the grill and close the lid for a couple of minutes for similar results.

HOT & COLD SMOKING

A subtle smoky texture is imparted by smoking. If you don't have a counter-top smoker, like mine, use a heavy-based saucepan and steamer with a tight-fitting lid. Line the saucepan with kitchen foil and a layer of wood chips, sit the steamer on top and put your chicken breast on a heatproof plate inside, then seal tightly and smoke over a low heat for 20–25 minutes. The cold smoking method doesn't use heat to cook the meat but just adds the flavour of the smoking ingredients so if you buy cold-smoked chicken, you still need to cook it before eating.

ROASTING

Whole chickens or bigger pieces of meat come into their own when roasting. They are sometimes cooked quickly at a higher temperature, or they can be sealed first at a high temperature, then finished more slowly. This combination again achieves the ideal option of crisp skin and moist and tender meat.

SLOW COOKING

Slow cooking chicken in the oven or on the hob almost guarantees succulent results, and slow-cooked casseroles give superb results, especially for leg and thigh meat, as the long cooking time allows the meat to break down gradually and tenderize while merging with the flavours of the sauce ingredients. You can also slow cook the leg meat in oil.

POACHING & STEAMING

Also on the hob, you can poach chicken in milk, stock or water, bringing the poaching liquid to the boil, then reducing it to a gentle simmer. It is ideal for any type or cut of chicken, although especially good for keeping breast meat moist, and, as you don't use any fat in the cooking process, it's a healthy way to cook. Cooking chicken in a steamer over a pan of simmering water is another healthy method that gives succulent results. Both poached and steamed chicken are often finished off by pan-frying, just to give the meat that attractive bit of colour that is lacking in steamed or poached meat.

SOUS-VIDE

Popular in the restaurant industry for many years but only recently in the home, cooking chicken sous-vide means vacuum-sealing the meat, then cooking it in a water bath at 70°C/150°F. Restaurants use a vacuum-sealer and a special bath but you can wrap the meat tightly in cling film and kitchen foil, then cook it in a pan of water for about an hour, maintaining an even temperature, and finish it in a hot pan. The method can be used on all cuts of meat, retaining all the cooking juices.

about the recipes

'If you do what you've always done, you'll get what you've always got.' That's something I heard years ago and it's as true in the kitchen as in any walk of life. Cooking is about developing your knowledge of food, understanding what makes the finest ingredients, learning how to use the right utensils, practising your skills and – most of all – developing your own ideas and creating new dishes. And that's what I hope this book will help you to achieve.

I've put together a collection of recipes that put chicken centre stage and explore its potential, using all different cuts and cooking methods, flavours and combinations. You'll find the classics here, of course, but I've looked at every recipe with new eyes to give each one a modern twist, and show you imaginative and highly contemporary recipes that will offer you meals for every occasion, from street-smart snacks to dishes to wow your guests at your next dinner party.

But recipes don't work in isolation. To become favourites, they must respond to our lives. Dinner in our house most of the time involves putting something together quickly that tastes great and that everyone will enjoy – including the kids. At the weekends, I want to be a bit more relaxed, while when we have guests, I am cooking to impress. That's why I have divided the recipes into three lifetsyle-focused chapters: Weekday Meals, For the Weekend and Dinners & Celebrations.

WEEKDAY MEALS

Quick and easy is my weekday mantra – recipes focused on the days when life takes over and we seem to be constantly in a rush. With work, school, clubs and daily chores, we often have to fit mealtimes into the odd spaces that are left, and this chapter is packed with meals that fit that space neatly. If you are lucky, you may have an odd moment, either during the week or at the weekend, to prepare some dishes in advance to help things flow more smoothly – perhaps a casserole or a couple of child-friendly snacks.

If you are looking for a light lunch, you'll find loads of choices, like Chargrilled Chicken, Fennel & Feta Salad (see page 33), Thai-Style Chicken Broth & Soba Noodles (see page 28) or Marcus's Ultimate Club Sandwich (see page 52). If it's something more substantial you are looking for, my Chicken, Basil Pesto & Courgette Risotto (see page 61) won't disappoint – there's even a make-ahead, time-saving tip. There are lots of recipes to suit all the family, from my Spice-Rubbed, Roasted Half Chicken with Smoky Bacon Chips (see page 74) to Chicken, Leek & Cream Linguine (see page 69).

FOR THE WEEKEND

The weekend may be more relaxed, but you still have plenty to do, so as well as some more creative dishes that demand a bit more time, there are Sunday roasts, things for the kids and some wonderful comfort foods. For a light meal, try my Chicken, Lemongrass & Thyme Scotch Eggs with Mustard Mayonnaise (see page 82). I have been refining this recipe for some years and now I feel I have got it spot on, with the perfect crispy coating around the tasty mince with a zesty zing of lemongrass to complement the thyme, and the runny yolk in the centre. In my house, Chicken, Chorizo & Butterbean Casserole (see page 109) is a favouite, but we also love the pies, pastas, curries and quiches – and I'm sure you will, too.

DINNERS & CELEBRATIONS

Presentation and impact are key to impressing your friends with your culinary skills. You want things to look and taste great, but you want to enjoy the party, too, so the dishes in the final section fulfil both criteria – they are packed with plenty of the wow factor but are surprisingly quick to prepare. I'm a big fan of starters as if you spend the time to get the presentation and flavour right, you start your meal on the right note. Try Poached Chicken, Mango & Asparagus Verrine (see page 149) or Vietnamese Chicken & Pomegranate Seed Wraps with Sweet Chilli Sauce (see page 161). Then balance the flavours in your starter with your main course. For a modern twist here, see how well flavours from different cuisines work together, as in Chargrilled Chicken Tikka on Lemongrass Sticks, which I serve with chicory and tomatoes (see page 185).

FEATURE RECIPES

Each section also includes feature recipes that show off some of the classic partners to cook with chicken, marrying them together in unexpected ways. If you love the combination of chicken and mushrooms, Asian Chicken & Mushroom Ballotines (see page 172) will show them in a new light. Everyone loves chicken and chips, but you'll never have tasted anything quite like my modern all-in-one version – Crispy Chicken & Potato Crust (see page 70).

Hopefully, these features will encourage you to start experimenting with your own dishes, substituting your favourite ingredients or adapting recipes to the seasons or the ingredients to hand. Cooking is about experimenting with flavours and finding out what works. I've created recipes to start you off, but don't ever be scared of trying to combine flavours and textures and trying something new. It's what makes you a great cook! So now you have been introduced to the stars of the show, nothing remains but to head for the kitchen and start cooking.

1

weekday meals

Thai-style chicken broth & soba noodles

This recipe is a great example of a dish with stacks of flavour that is also really good for you. If you feel a cold coming on, you'll soon be back fighting fit if you make yourself a steaming bowl of this powerful broth with its medicinal properties.

Bring the stock to the boil in a large saucepan over a high heat. Finely slice and mince the lower portion of the lemongrass stalk and put the top in the stock whole. Add the ginger, lime leaves, fish sauce, mirin, soy sauce, vinegar, chilli, lime juice and bonito flakes and stir well. Turn the heat down to low and simmer for 5 minutes.

Meanwhile, bring a saucepan of water to the boil over a high heat. Add the soba noodles, return to the boil and cook for 5 minutes, then drain the noodles and put them in a bowl of ice-cold water to stop them cooking further. Leave in the water until required.

Dust the chicken in the cornflour, then add to the broth, stirring. Add the spring onions and coriander and simmer for 4–5 minutes until the chicken is cooked through.

Drain the soba noodles and add to the pan. Simmer for a further 2 minutes until hot before serving.

Serves 4
Preparation time: 20 minutes, plus making the stock
Cooking time: 15 minutes

800ml/28fl oz/scant 3½ cups Chicken Stock (see page 197)

1 lemongrass stalk

5cm/2in piece of root ginger, peeled and finely sliced into matchstick-sized pieces

2 kaffir lime leaves

1 tbsp Thai fish sauce

2 tbsp mirin

2 tbsp light soy sauce

1 tbsp rice wine vinegar

1 red chilli, deseeded and finely sliced into rings

juice of ½ lime

2 tbsp dried bonito flakes

200g/7oz soba noodles

2 skinless chicken breasts, finely sliced into strips

2 tsp cornflour

4 spring onions, finely sliced into rings

2 tbsp coriander leaves

Chicken Waterzooi

The Belgians are primarily known for their mussels and French fries, but this is a less well-known, traditional Belgian recipe for chicken. It's a rich, chunky soup that will keep you going throughout the day. You can also try it with fish instead of chicken.

Heat the oil and butter in a frying pan over a medium heat. Add the chicken and cook for 1–2 minutes until just coloured. Add the onions, garlic, carrots and leek and cook for 3–4 minutes until lightly coloured.

Add the stock and cream, turn the heat down to low and simmer for 20–30 minutes until the vegetables are tender and the sauce has reduced slightly.

Put the egg yolk in a bowl and slowly whisk in a little of the soup until blended, then stir the mixture back into the soup. Stir in the chopped herbs and season with salt and pepper to taste.

Serve the hot soup with chunks of crusty bread.

Serves 4
Preparation time: 15 minutes,
   plus making the stock
Cooking time: 35 minutes

1 tbsp olive oil
1 tbsp unsalted butter
2 skinless chicken breasts, diced
2 onions, finely diced
2 garlic cloves, chopped
2 carrots, peeled and finely diced
1 large leek, trimmed, halved and sliced
500ml/17fl oz/2 cups Chicken Stock
   (see page 197)
100ml/3½fl oz/scant ½ cup double cream
1 large egg yolk
2 tbsp chopped parsley leaves
1 tbsp chopped chives
1 tbsp chopped tarragon leaves
sea salt and freshly ground black pepper
crusty bread, to serve

Winter chicken Waldorf salad with crispy shallots

A winter version of the classic salad, this combines some excellent flavours from the coldest season. Make sure you choose some lovely juicy apples that are crisp and full of flavour, and top it off with some of my crispy fried shallots.

Preheat the grill to medium-high. Season the chicken with salt and pepper, put in a baking tin and grill for 6–7 minutes on each side, turning frequently, until the juices run clear when the thickest part of the chicken is pierced with the tip of a sharp knife.

Put all the salad ingredients in a bowl and toss together lightly. Chop the chicken into chunks and add to the salad ingredients.

Whisk together all the dressing ingredients in a separate bowl. Spoon a little of the dressing over the salad and gently toss together. Top with the crispy shallots to serve.

Serves 4
Preparation time: 15 minutes,
  plus making the mayonnaise
Cooking time: 15 minutes

3 skinless chicken breasts
3 red juicy apples, such as Pink Lady,
  cored and cut into small wedges
4 celery sticks, finely chopped
20 walnut halves, toasted
50g/1¾oz watercress
sea salt and freshly ground black pepper
1 recipe quantity Crispy Fried Shallots
  (see page 205), to serve

FOR THE WALDORF DRESSING
2 tbsp walnut oil
1 tsp sherry vinegar
3 tbsp Mayonnaise (see page 202)
1 tsp Dijon mustard
½ tsp lemon juice

Chargrilled chicken, fennel & feta salad

Simple salads make great lunches. Fresh, easy to put together, very healthy and with loads of flavours, you really can't go wrong. If you can grow a few herbs in your garden or on the window sill, you'll always have a fresh supply.

Rub a little oil all over the chicken pieces, then season with a little salt and pepper. Heat a griddle pan over a high heat until smoking, or use a barbecue. Add the chicken to the griddle pan and cook for 3–4 minutes on each side until the juices run clear when the thickest part of the chicken is pierced with the tip of a sharp knife. Leave to one side.

Meanwhile, put all the remaining ingredients except the dressing in a bowl and toss together lightly. Slice the chicken and add it to the salad, then toss again. Drizzle with the dressing just before serving.

Serves 4
Preparation time: 5 minutes,
  plus making the dressing
Cooking time: 10 minutes

a little olive oil
4 skinlesss chicken breasts, sliced
  in half lengthways
100g/3^{1}/2oz salad leaves
150g/5^{1}/2oz/1 cup podded peas
2 small fennel bulbs, sliced into thin
  strips using a vegetable peeler
leaves from 4 dill sprigs, roughly chopped
leaves from 4 mint sprigs, roughly
  chopped
150g/5^{1}/2oz feta cheese, crumbled
2 tbsp Bean House Salad Dressing
  (see page 203)
sea salt and freshly ground black pepper

Glazed orange & mustard chicken salad

There's a lovely contrast of tastes and textures in this dish, with the freshness of the orange contrasting with the rich mustard flavour. If you toss the chicken in the marinade before you go to work, it will take no time at all to put it together when you get home. For a more substantial dish, you could add parmentier potatoes, sprinkling them over just before serving.

Preheat the oven to 200°C/400°F/Gas 6. Mix together all the marinade ingredients in a non-metallic bowl. Season the chicken breasts with salt and pepper, then add to the bowl and toss the chicken in the marinade. Cover with cling film and leave to marinate in the fridge for 30 minutes.

Put the chicken in a roasting tin and roast for 25 minutes, basting occasionally with a little of the marinade, until the juices run clear when the thickest part of the chicken is pierced with the tip of a sharp knife. If the chicken is getting too brown, cover it with kitchen foil until it has finished cooking.

Mix together the chard and baby spinach, season with salt and pepper to taste and drizzle over a little of the dressing. Toss together well. Serve the chicken and salad with parmentier potatoes.

Serves 4
Preparation time: 10 minutes, plus 30 minutes marinating, and making the dressing
Cooking time: 25 minutes

4 skinless chicken breasts
12 chard leaves, finely chopped
100g/3½oz baby spinach leaves
2 tbsp Bean House Salad Dressing (see page 203)
sea salt and freshly ground black pepper
1 recipe quantity Parmentier Potatoes (see page 214) or new potatoes, to serve

FOR THE ORANGE & MUSTARD MARINADE
2 tbsp orange marmalade
1 garlic clove, crushed and finely diced
1 tbsp Dijon mustard
1 tbsp wholegrain mustard
grated zest and juice of ½ orange
1 tbsp olive oil
1 tbsp sherry vinegar

Quinoa, chicken & asparagus salad

I always remember my mum making a pie with this classic combination of chicken with asparagus. I have tried to give this great combo a new modern take to highlight the subtle contrasts in flavour and texture, so I've kept the asparagus raw and peeled it thinly into strips, then used it in a salad with that fantastic, much-under-used grain, quinoa. This makes for a really healthy dish that I'm sure you will enjoy.

Bring a saucepan of water to the boil over a high heat. Add the quinoa and return to the boil. Turn the heat down to low and simmer for 10–15 minutes until tender. Drain through a fine sieve, then leave to dry out for a couple of minutes.

Meanwhile, put the chicken in a bowl, pour in the oil and season with salt and pepper. Toss together to coat the chicken in the oil. Heat a chargill pan, then add the chicken and cook for 5 minutes on each side until browned and the juices run clear when the thickest part of the chicken is pierced with the tip of a sharp knife. Remove from the grill pan and leave to rest for a few minutes, then cut the chicken into thick slices.

Put the quinoa in a bowl and add the chives and orange zest and juice. Season with salt and pepper to taste, then pile onto plates. Mix together the asparagus and carrot strips and pile on top of the quinoa. Top with the chicken, then scatter with the spring onions and serve.

Serves 4
Preparation time: 15 minutes
Cooking time: 15 minutes

120g/4.¼oz/scant ⅔ cup quinoa
4 skinless chicken breasts
2 tbsp olive oil
3 tbsp chopped chives
grated zest and juice of ½ orange
12 asparagus stems, cut into long, thin
  strips using a vegetable peeler
2 carrots, peeled and cut into long, thin
  strips using a vegetable peeler
8 spring onions, finely sliced into strips
sea salt and freshly ground black pepper

Thai-style chicken yuk sung

Yuk sung is a fresh and simple dish, but I always feel it could do with a bit more spice. So my version of the recipe uses chicken and Thai spices combined with sweet mango to give it a great flavour. It is ideal as a snack or starter or a sharing course for friends.

Mix together the mango, mint and lime leaf in a bowl, cover and chill in the fridge while you cook the chicken.

Heat half the oil in a large frying pan over a high heat until shimmering. Add the chicken and cook for 2 minutes, stirring continuously. Remove the meat from the pan using a slotted spoon, put on a plate and leave to one side.

Heat the remaining oil and fry the garlic, chilli and ginger for 1 minute. Add the lemongrass and fry for another minute, then return the chicken to the pan along with the juices on the plate and mix everything together. Add the dark soy sauce, fish sauce, sugar and coriander and mix thoroughly until hot.

Remove from the heat and spoon the mixture into the lettuce leaves, piling it as high as you can. Top with the mango mixture and serve.

Serves 4
Preparation time: 10 minutes
Cooking time: 5 minutes

½ mango, peeled, pitted and finely diced
4 mint leaves, roughly chopped
1 kaffir lime leaf, finely shredded
2 tbsp groundnut oil
2 skinless boneless chicken thighs, roughly chopped
2 garlic cloves, roughly chopped
½ red chilli, including the seeds, roughly chopped
5cm/2in piece of root ginger, peeled and roughly chopped
1 lemongrass stalk, peeled and finely chopped
½ tbsp dark soy sauce
½ tbsp Thai fish sauce
1 tsp palm sugar
2 tbsp finely chopped coriander leaves
8 small Little Gem lettuce leaves

Crispy sesame chicken strips with sweet & sour sauce

For this recipe, I use strips of chicken breast – known as inner fillets – cut from the underside of the breast. You can buy chicken fillets or cut one fillet from each chicken breast, then use the breasts for another recipe. You can make the sweet and sour sauce while the chicken is chilling.

Put the flour on a shallow plate and season with plenty of salt and pepper.

Mix together the breadcrumbs and sesame seeds on a second shallow plate. Whisk together the eggs and milk in a third shallow plate to make an egg wash, then line the three plates up in a row. Lightly dust each chicken fillet in the flour, shaking off any excess. Dip in the egg wash, then coat with the breadcrumbs. Put them on a plate, cover lightly with cling film and chill in the fridge for at least 10 minutes or until ready to use.

Heat the oil in a large, heavy-based frying pan over a medium heat, to 170°C/325°F, when a cube of bread browns in 60 seconds. Carefully put the fillets in the pan and cook for 2–3 minutes on each side until cooked through and golden brown.

Drain the fillets on kitchen paper to remove any excess oil, then serve with the sweet and sour sauce and a herb salad.

Serves 4
Preparation time: 10 minutes,
   plus at least 10 minutes chilling
Cooking time: 10 minutes

50g/1¾oz/heaped ⅓ cup plain flour
75g/2½oz/¾ cup panko breadcrumbs
4 tbsp sesame seeds
2 eggs, beaten
3 tbsp milk
10 skinless chicken inner fillets
150ml/5fl oz/scant ⅔ cup groundnut oil
sea salt and freshly ground black pepper
1 recipe quantity Sweet & Sour Sauce
   (see page 200), to serve
1 recipe quantity Herb Salad (see page
   219), to serve

Chicken spring rolls with hoisin sauce

I don't always feel hungry after I've finished cooking, and at those times I just want a selection of little bites to eat. That's when these spring rolls really hit the spot, especially served with my homemade hoisin sauce. The kids love them, too, and they are much better for them than the shop-bought versions. You can buy spring roll wrappers in most Asian food stores.

Heat the olive oil in a frying pan over a medium heat. Add the chicken and fry for 4–5 minutes, stirring to break up the mince, until browned and cooked through. Transfer to a bowl and leave to cool for 3–4 minutes. Stir in the carrots, bean sprouts and soy sauce and season with salt and pepper to taste. Whisk together the eggs, milk and a pinch of salt to make an egg wash.

Take 2 spring roll wrappers, one on top of the other. Put 2 tablespoons of the meat mixture in the centre, brush a little of the egg wash around the edges, then fold over each end and roll up. Seal with a little egg wash on the join and leave to one side. Repeat until you have made 4 rolls.

Heat the groundnut oil in a deep, heavy-based saucepan to 170°C/325°F, when a cube of bread browns in 60 seconds. Add the spring rolls, a few at a time if necessary, and cook for 1–2 minutes until golden, then remove from the oil and drain on kitchen paper for 1 minute. Serve hot with the hoisin sauce and a microleaf salad.

Serves 4
Preparation time: 15 minutes, plus making the hoisin sauce
Cooking time: 10 minutes

2 tbsp olive oil
500g/1lb 2oz minced chicken
2 carrots, peeled and cut into matchstick-sized pieces
120g/4¼oz bean sprouts
2 tbsp light soy sauce
2 eggs
2 tsp milk
2 packets of spring roll wrappers
groundnut oil, for deep-frying
sea salt and freshly ground black pepper
1 recipe quantity Hoisin Sauce (see page 200), to serve
1 recipe quantity Microleaf & Carrot Salad (see page 219), to serve

Chicken fajitas & homemade smoked paprika wraps

Fajitas have always been my choice for an informal meal with friends and before I started cooking, we'd make them straight from the pack. But once I started to cook I wanted to make my perfect feast even better by cooking everything from scratch – and it's so worth it. Plus fajitas are so quick to make, they are great for midweek meals for your family or when you invite a few friends round for supper. Your friends are sure to be impressed – and they'll enjoy it all the more if you stock up on a few bottles of Mexican lager to wash it down.

Put the chicken in a bowl, drizzle with the oil and season with salt and pepper.

Heat a griddle pan over a high heat until it just starts to smoke, then add the chicken, in batches if necessary, and cook for 1–2 minutes on each side until it has charred markings. Repeat with the peppers.

Serve the chicken and peppers with the wraps, soured cream, salsa and guacamole so your guests can wrap and enjoy their own fajitas.

Serves 4
Preparation time: 10 minutes, plus making the wraps, salsa and guacamole
Cooking time: 20 minutes

4 skinless chicken breasts, cut into 8 even-sized strips
2 tbsp olive oil
1 red pepper, deseeded and cut into strips
1 green pepper, deseeded and cut into strips
sea salt and freshly ground black pepper

TO SERVE
1 recipe quantity Smoked Paprika Wraps (see page 209)
4 tbsp soured cream
1 recipe quantity Tomato Salsa (see page 201)
1 recipe quantity Guacamole (see page 201)

Mango & coriander coronation chicken pitta pockets

Coronation chicken is a great British classic, with its balance of spicy and sweet Anglo-Indian flavours. I love making my own curry powder so I can make it as spicy or aromatic as I want. Once the mixture is made, it will keep in the fridge for 4–5 days. Those who like to take a healthy and nutritious lunch to work need look no further as these make the perfect portable lunch.

Put all the spices in a small saucepan over a medium heat for about 4 minutes until they just start to warm through and release a spicy aroma. Tip into a small spice grinder or pestle and mortar and grind until you have a fine powder.

Add a teaspoonful of the curry powder to the mayonnaise and season with salt and pepper to taste. Add more curry powder to the mayonnaise, if you like. Fold in the chicken.

Preheat the grill and toast the pitta breads on both sides, then cut each one across widthways to make 2 pitta pockets. Fill them with the coronation chicken mixture, then top with the mango and coriander. Eat on their own as a quick snack or with homemade sweet potato crisps.

Serves 4
Preparation time: 10 minutes, plus making the mayonnaise
Cooking time: 5 minutes

3–4 tbsp Mayonnaise (see page 202)
500g/1lb 2oz poached skinless chicken breasts (see page 23), shredded or cut into chunks
4 wholemeal or white pitta breads
1 ripe mango, peeled, pitted and diced
40g/1$\frac{1}{2}$oz coriander leaves, chopped
sea salt and freshly ground black pepper
1 recipe quantity Sweet Potato Crisps (see page 215), to serve

FOR THE CURRY POWDER
$\frac{1}{2}$ tsp ground cardamom
$\frac{1}{2}$ star anise
1 tbsp coriander seeds
1 tbsp turmeric
$\frac{1}{2}$ tbsp fenugreek seeds
1 tbsp ground cumin
2 tsp mustard seeds
$\frac{1}{2}$ tsp fennel seeds
1 tsp dried chilli flakes
1 tbsp olive oil

Chicken, tomato & rocket pesto arancini

A delicious risotto-style mixture, coated in breadcrumbs and fried until golden, arancini are a Sicilian speciality that uses up risotto that you made in too generous portions. Hot or cold, they make the perfect snack food for a busy day – filling, fresh and full of flavour.

Put the risotto in a bowl and mix in the chicken, tomatoes and a spoonful of pesto. Season with salt and pepper to taste. Shape the rice mixture into about 8 small balls.

Whisk together the eggs and milk in a shallow bowl to make an egg wash. Put the breadcrumbs and Parmesan in another shallow bowl. One at a time, dip the arancini in the egg wash, coating all sides, then shake off any excess and roll in the cheese breadcrumbs until coated.

Heat the oil in a deep, heavy-based saucepan to 170°C/ 325°F, when a cube of day-old bread will brown in 60 seconds. Gently lower the arancini, one at a time, into the hot oil and cook for about 3 minutes until golden.

Drain on kitchen paper, then serve with extra pesto for dipping. They make delicious canapés for drinks parties, are lovely as a starter, or you can serve them with a mixed salad for a light lunch or dinner.

Serves 4
Preparation time: 15 minutes, plus 30 minutes cooling, and making the slow-roasted tomatoes and pesto
Cooking time: 25 minutes

250g/9oz/heaped 1 cup leftover risotto rice or risotto base (see page 61), chilled
1–2 poached or roasted chicken breasts (see page 23), skinned, shredded and finely chopped
60g/2¼oz Slow-Roasted Tomatoes (see page 218), drained and finely chopped
1–2 tbsp Fresh Rocket Pesto (see page 201), plus extra to serve
2 eggs, beaten
a small splash of milk
250g/9oz/2½ cups panko breadcrumbs
50g/1¾oz Parmesan cheese, grated
groundnut oil, for deep-frying
sea salt and freshly ground black pepper

Chicken falafel with cucumber raita

The simplest dishes often give the best results and this fits the bill. I've made it from scratch for this recipe but it is also a good way to use leftover cooked chicken from your Sunday roast – just leave out the first step and start by blitzing your falafel ingredients.

Bring the stock to the boil in a saucepan over a medium heat. Add the chicken, turn the heat down to low and simmer for 15–20 minutes until the juices run clear when the thickest part of the chicken is pierced with the tip of a sharp knife. Drain, then shred the chicken with two forks while it is still hot.

Put all the falafel ingredients except the chicken into a blender and blitz until well blended. Tip into a bowl, add the chicken, season with salt and pepper and mix together. Use your hands to shape into about 24 small balls, then dust with flour.

Heat the oil in a deep, heavy-based saucepan to 170°C/ 325°F, when a cube of bread browns in 60 seconds. Fry the falafels for about 4 minutes until golden brown. Remove using a slotted spoon and drain on kitchen paper.

Meanwhile, put the yogurt in a bowl, stir in the mint and cucumber and season with salt and pepper to taste.

Serve the chicken falafels and yogurt with a tomato, feta, onion and mint salad.

Serves: 4
Preparation time: 15 minutes, plus overnight soaking, and making the stock
Cooking time: 25 minutes

300ml/10½fl oz/scant 1¼ cups Chicken Stock (see page 197)
3 skinless chicken breasts, quartered
400g/14oz/heaped 1¾ cups dried chickpeas, soaked overnight, then drained
1 onion, finely chopped
2 garlic cloves
1 tbsp gram flour
1 tbsp ground cumin
2 tbsp chopped coriander leaves
seeds from ½ black cardamom pod
¼ tsp cayenne pepper
½ tsp turmeric
2 tbsp tahini paste
300g/10½oz cooked sweet potato
1 egg yolk
a little plain flour, for dusting
groundnut oil, for deep-frying
sea salt and freshly ground black pepper
tomato, feta, red onion and mint salad, to serve

FOR THE CUCUMBER RAITA
200g/7oz/scant 1 cup natural yogurt
2 tbsp chopped mint leaves
50g/1¾oz cucumber, peeled, deseeded and grated

Smoky bacon chicken wings

If you have been browsing through my recipes, you may have already noticed that pancetta is one of my favourite ingredients – the slow curing process gives it such a fantastic flavour that goes so well with chicken, which absorbs the strong flavours and somehow seems to improve on them. There are so many recipes for chicken wrapped in bacon that I wanted to add a new twist, so I've cooked the pancetta in the oven until crisp, then mixed it with sugar and spice to make a bacon rub to add to the chicken wings and transform them into a tasty, spicy snack.

Preheat the oven to 200°C/400°F/Gas 6. Put the strips of pancetta on a baking tray and bake for 15 minutes until dark and crisp. Remove from the oven and leave to cool.

Put into a spice grinder or blender and blitz to a powder, then add the sugar, smoked paprika and cayenne and blitz quickly again.

Put the chicken wings in a bowl and rub all the smoky bacon mixture into the wings. Spread them out on a baking tray, making sure there is plenty of the bacon mixture on top of the wings so it melts as they cook. Roast for 20 minutes until the chicken wings are coloured and cooked through. Serve warm on their own as a smoky and spicy snack.

Serves 4
Preparation time: 10 minutes
Cooking time: 35 minutes

8 strips of pancetta
2 tsp dark soft brown sugar
2 tsp smoked paprika
½ tsp cayenne pepper
16 chicken wings

Southern fried chicken & chilli corn

Delicious, inexpensive and easy to make, I think just about everyone must have tried this at one time or another but perhaps not made it for themselves. There's no reason to be hesitant as you can follow this simple recipe to make the perfect crisp chicken with a side of chilli corn.

Put the chicken pieces in a bowl. Mix together the buttermilk and Tabasco sauce, pour over the chicken and turn to mix together. Cover with cling film and leave to marinate in the fridge for 8 hours or overnight.

Drain the chicken pieces, reserving the buttermilk in a shallow bowl. Preheat the oven to 180°C/350°F/Gas 4. Heat 4cm/1½in of oil in a heavy-based saucepan over a medium heat to 160–180°C/315–350°F, when a cube of bread browns in 60 seconds.

While the oil is heating, mix the flour with the spices and herbs in a shallow bowl. Dip the first chicken piece in the buttermilk, shake off any excess, then coat all over in the flour. Lower into the hot oil and fry for 2–3 minutes until golden in colour. As it is cooking, continue with the next piece, adding them to the pan in a clockwise direction so you know which will be finished first. As each piece is cooked, transfer to a baking tray using a slotted spoon. When they are all cooked, place in the oven and bake for 5–10 minutes, or until the coating is crisp and golden brown and the juices run clear when the thickest part is pierced with the tip of a sharp knife.

Meanwhile, bring a large saucepan of water to the boil over a high heat. Add the corn and return to the boil. Cook for 5 minutes, then drain.

Put the butter and chilli in a bowl, season well with salt and pepper and mix together. Smear the cobs with the chilli butter and serve with the chicken pieces.

Serves 4
Preparation time: 10 minutes,
  plus overnight marinating
Cooking time: 20 minutes

12 chicken drumsticks or thighs, skin on
500ml/17fl oz/2 cups buttermilk
1 tsp Tabasco sauce
olive oil, for deep-frying
150g/5½oz/1¼ cups self-raising flour
2 tbsp smoked paprika
1 tbsp sea salt
1 tbsp freshly ground black pepper
1 tsp cayenne pepper
1 tsp chilli powder
2 tsp chopped thyme leaves
4 corn cobs, cut into chunks
50g/1¾oz unsalted butter
1 red chilli, deseeded and finely chopped

Marcus's ultimate club sandwich

Sometimes I crave nothing more than a good sandwich and, of course, the club sandwich is the ultimate. For the best results, use homemade toasted bread or a freshly baked artisan bread from a local bakery. Chicken and smoked bacon are a great combination and with slow-roasted tomatoes and the avocado salsa, it works just perfectly.

Preheat the oven to 220°C/425°F/Gas 7. Put the bacon on a baking tray and bake for 15–20 minutes until just crisp. Leave to one side until required. Turn the oven down to 200°C/400°F/Gas 6.

Season the chicken with a little salt. Heat the oil in a large, ovenproof saucepan over a medium-high heat. Add the chicken and cook for 2–3 minutes on each side until just browned. Transfer the pan to the oven and cook for 15–20 minutes until the juices run clear when the thickest part of the chicken is pierced with the tip of a sharp knife. (Omit this step if you are using cooked chicken.)

To make the avocado salsa, cut the avocado in half, discard the pit and scoop out all the flesh into a bowl. Squeeze in the lime juice, then crush with the back of a fork to make a paste. Stir in the coriander and season with salt and pepper to taste.

Toast the bread on both sides and butter the slices on one side. Take 4 slices of bread and spread a layer of mayonnaise on the buttered side of each one, then put 2 slices of bacon on each slice, spread the red onion on top and spoon over the slow-roasted tomatoes. Put another slice of buttered bread on top of each pile, then spread the tops with half the avocado mixture. Slice the chicken and put on the top, then add the rocket, season with a little salt and pepper, then top with the remaining slices of bread, buttered-side down.

Gently press the sandwiches to pack them down, then cut them in half and pierce each half with a skewer to hold them together. Serve with the remaining avocado salsa and with homemade sweet potato crisps, if you like.

Serves 4
Preparation time: 15 minutes, plus making the mayonnaise and slow-roasted tomatoes
Cooking time: 40 minutes

8 smoked back bacon rashers
4 skinless chicken breasts, or use leftover cooked chicken
1 tbsp olive oil
12 slices of homemade or artisan bread
50g/1¾oz salted butter, at room temperature
4 tbsp Mayonnaise (see page 202)
250g/9oz Slow-Roasted Tomatoes (see page 218)
1 small red onion, thinly sliced
40g/1½oz rocket leaves
sea salt and freshly ground black pepper
1 recipe quantity Sweet Potato Crisps (see page 215), to serve (optional)

FOR THE AVOCADO SALSA
1 ripe avocado
½ lime
1 tsp chopped coriander leaves

Chicken & slow-roasted tomato burgers with pesto mayonnaise

I do love a good burger. My tip for success is to build on the flavour of the minced chicken, starting with the onion and garlic, then adding herbs and sauces. My special ingredient in this burger is the slow-roasted tomatoes, which lift the flavour and give a lovely, fresh kick. Combine it with the fresh basil pesto mayonnaise and you have something really special.

Preheat the oven to 200°C/400°F/Gas 6. Put the minced chicken in a bowl and add the tomatoes, onion, garlic, thyme, truffle oil, breadcrumbs and Worcestershire and Tabasco sauces and mix well until combined. Shape into 4 burgers, then cover and chill in the fridge for 20 minutes to firm up while you cook the sweet potato wedges.

Meanwhile, mix together the pesto and mayonnaise, cover and chill in the fridge until ready to use.

Heat the olive oil in a griddle pan or frying pan over a medium-high heat. Add the burgers and cook for 3–4 minutes on each side until browned, turning the heat down to low if they start to brown too quickly. Transfer to the oven and cook for 5–10 minutes with the sweet potatoes until cooked through and browned.

Remove the burgers from the oven, cover and leave to rest in a warm place while you toast the bread rolls. Put some rocket leaves on the bottom half of each bun, top with a spoonful of the pesto mayonnaise, then the burger, another spoonful of pesto mayonnaise, then the remaining bun. Serve with the sweet potato wedges.

Serves 4
Preparation time: 20 minutes, plus 20 minutes chilling, and making the slow-roasted tomatoes, pesto and mayonnaise
Cooking time: 30 minutes

600g/1lb 5oz minced chicken
300g/10½oz Slow-Roasted Tomatoes (see page 218) or sun-dried tomatoes (not in oil), finely chopped
1 onion, diced
2 garlic bulbs, crushed and chopped
leaves from 2 thyme sprigs, chopped
2 tsp truffle oil
2 tbsp breadcrumbs
2 tsp Worcestershire sauce
½ tsp Tabasco sauce
1 tbsp olive oil
4 bread rolls, sliced in half
1 handful of rocket leaves
sea salt and freshly ground black pepper
1 recipe quantity Sweet Potato Wedges (see page 215), to serve

FOR THE PESTO MAYONNAISE
2 tbsp Fresh Basil Pesto (see page 201)
4 tbsp Mayonnaise (see page 202)

Chicken schnitzel with sorrel mayonnaise

A schnitzel is a boneless piece of meat that has been flattened out, then egg washed, breadcrumbed and fried. The dish originated in Austria and Germany and traditionally would have used veal. I really enjoy a bit of fried chicken and the beauty of this recipe is it is super-quick to cook and the chicken stays really tender. Plus you can serve it with any kind of potatoes and vegetables. The delicious sorrel mayonnaise gives it a contemporary twist.

Place each chicken breast between two layers of cling film and use a rolling pin to bash them until they are about 1.5cm/⅝in thick.

Put the flour on a shallow plate and season with plenty of salt and pepper. Mix together the breadcrumbs, fennel seeds and rosemary on a second shallow plate. Whisk together the eggs and milk in a third shallow plate, then line the three plates up in a row. Lightly dust each chicken breast in the flour, shaking off any excess. Dip in the egg, then coat with the breadcrumbs. Put them on a plate, cover lightly with cling film and chill in the fridge for 10 minutes, or until required.

Meanwhile, heat the oil in a large frying pan over a medium-high heat. If your pan will not hold all the schnitzels comfortably, cook them in batches. Gently put the schnitzels in the pan and cook for 2–3 minutes on each side until cooked through and golden brown.

Mix the sorrel and lemon juice into the mayonnaise, then season with salt and pepper to taste. Serve the chicken and sorrel mayonnaise with sweet potato wedges and some green beans.

Serves 4
Preparation time: 30 minutes, plus 10 minutes chilling, and making the mayonnaise
Cooking time: 15 minutes

4 skinless chicken breasts
50g/1¾oz/scant ½ cup plain flour
150g/5½oz/1½ cups panko breadcrumbs
1 tsp fennel seeds
1 tsp chopped rosemary leaves
2 eggs, beaten
6 tbsp milk
80ml/2½fl oz/ ⅓ cup olive oil
sea salt and freshly ground black pepper
1 recipe quantity Sweet Potato Wedges (see page 215), to serve
steamed green beans, to serve

FOR THE SORREL MAYONNAISE
4 tbsp chopped sorrel leaves or spinach leaves
juice of 1 lemon
1 recipe quantity of Mayonnaise (see page 202)

Chicken & broccoli soufflé omelette

I'm a big fan of omelettes as they are so quick to make, plus they are great for using up all sorts of cooked or leftover ingredients – in this case, chicken and broccoli – making them perfect for a quick and easy midweek meal. (By the way, try steaming broccoli when you cook it to keep the lovely green colour.) Most of all, eggs are full of protein and really good for you. For this recipe, I've given it that modern tweak by using extra egg whites. This really lifts the omelette and makes it a lot lighter and fluffier.

Preheat the oven to 180°C/350°F/Gas 4 and cut out a circle of baking paper that will fit the inside of a large, ovenproof frying pan.

Whisk the eggs in a large bowl until light, then season with salt and pepper and add the chives. In a separate bowl, whisk the eggs whites, using an electric whisk (unless you're feeling energetic!), until soft peaks form. Carefully fold the egg whites into the beaten egg, using a large metal spoon, then stir in the chicken and broccoli.

Heat the butter and oil in a large ovenproof frying pan over a medium-high heat. When the pan is hot and the butter is foaming, add the egg mixture and cook for 2–3 minutes until the base is beginning to set, then sprinkle with the cheese and transfer the pan to the oven for 3–4 minutes until the soufflé omelette has risen and is just set in the centre. Turn out onto a plate or serve straight from the pan.

Serves 4
Preparation time: 10 minutes,
   plus making the confit
Cooking time: 7 minutes

8 eggs
2 tbsp chopped chives
4 egg whites
300g/10½oz Confit Chicken (see page 122), diced
300g/10½oz steamed broccoli, cut into tiny florets
2 tbsp unsalted butter
2 tbsp olive oil
60g/2¼oz strongly flavoured hard cheese, such as a mature Cheddar, grated
sea salt and freshly ground black pepper

Blackened chicken with Mediterranean vegetable couscous

Couscous makes the perfect partner for this spice-blackened chicken. If you pop the chicken in the fridge to marinate before you go to work, it will be ready to cook as soon as you get home, and even more full of flavour from a longer time marinating. Toasting the couscous in advance also adds to the nutty flavour.

Mix together all the marinade ingredients in a non-metallic bowl, add the chicken and turn it so it is coated in the marinade. Cover and leave to marinate in the fridge for at least 20 minutes.

Preheat the oven to 200°C/400°F/Gas 6. While the oven is heating, soak the couscous.

Remove the chicken from the marinade and put in a roasting tin. Roast for 15–20 minutes until blackened on the outside and the juices run clear when the thickest part of the chicken is pierced with the tip of a sharp knife.

Leave the chicken to rest for 2 minutes, then slice and serve on top of the couscous.

Serves 4
Preparation time: 25 minutes, plus
  at least 20 minutes marinating, and
  making the stock
Cooking time: 20 minutes

4 skinless chicken breasts, lightly scored
400ml/14fl oz/generous 1½ cups
  Vegetable Stock (see page 197)
1 recipe quantity Mediterranean Vegetable
  Couscous (see page 211)
sea salt and freshly ground black pepper

**FOR THE BLACKENED CHICKEN
  MARINADE**
1 tsp ground cumin
1 tsp ground fennel seeds
1 tsp smoked paprika
¼ tsp ground ginger
1 tbsp dark soft brown sugar
2 tbsp light soy sauce
1 tsp balsamic vinegar
1 tsp chopped thyme leaves
1 tbsp tomato purée
¼ tsp cayenne pepper

Chicken, basil pesto & courgette risotto

Once you master the basics of risotto, the options are endless. To make it easier on busy weekdays, you can make the base in advance, then finish it off just before serving. If you like, you could top it with some of my crispy fried shallots.

Heat the oil and butter in a large frying pan over a medium heat. Add the onion and garlic and fry for 5 minutes, stirring occasionally, until softened. Stir in the rice to coat it in the onion mixture. Pour in the wine and stir until it is absorbed by the rice.

Add a small ladleful of the hot stock and stir until the stock has been absorbed by the rice before adding the next ladleful. Add the courgette, then continue adding the stock for about 10 minutes, stirring so the rice cooks evenly, until you have used half of it. This is the risotto base and it can be left at this stage, if more convenient, and the dish finished later. If you want to do this, transfer the rice to a container with a lid and leave to cool completely. When cool, cover and chill in the fridge for up to 2 days.

To cook the chicken, preheat the oven to 180°C/350°F/ Gas 4. Heat the oil in an ovenproof frying pan over a medium-high heat. Season the chicken with salt and pepper, add to the pan and fry for 3 minutes on each side to colour, then transfer the pan to the oven and cook for 15 minutes until the juices run clear when the thickest part of the chicken is pierced with the tip of a sharp knife. Remove from the oven, cover and leave to rest for 2–3 minutes, then slice into strips.

To finish the risotto, reheat the reserved stock. Return the risotto base to the large pan over a medium-low heat. Continue to add the stock a ladleful at a time for about 10 minutes, stirring continuously, until the stock has been absorbed and the rice is tender but still retains some bite.

Stir the pesto and chicken into the rice, then stir in the cream, Parmesan and lemon juice and season with salt and pepper. Sprinkle with the chives and some extra Parmesan and serve with salad and crispy shallots, if you like.

Serves 4
Preparation time: 20 minutes, plus making the stock and pesto
Cooking time: 35 minutes

FOR THE RISOTTO BASE

1 tbsp olive oil
75g/2½oz unsalted butter
1 large onion, finely diced
2 garlic cloves, finely diced
250g/9oz/scant 1¼ cups risotto rice, such as Arborio
200ml/7fl oz/scant 1 cup dry white wine
750ml/26fl oz/3 cups hot Vegetable Stock (see page 197)
1 courgette, finely diced

FOR THE RISOTTO

2 tbsp olive oil
4 skinless chicken breasts
3–4 tbsp Fresh Basil Pesto (see page 201)
100ml/3½fl oz/scant ½ cup double cream
150g/5½oz Parmesan cheese, grated, plus extra for serving
juice and zest of ½ lemon
1 tbsp chives
sea salt and freshly ground black pepper

TO SERVE

Herb Salad (see page 219) or a Green Salad (see page 219)
1 recipe quantity Crispy Fried Shallots (see page 205) (optional)

Chicken, chorizo & tiger prawn paella

Sometimes you just want to cook a simple one-pot dish that will give you lots of flavour and feed lots of people. For those moments, this is the perfect recipe, and I guarantee the whole family will love it, even the kids. It's certainly a favourite with my daughters.

Heat the oil and butter in a large, non-stick frying pan over a medium heat. Add the onion and garlic and cook for 3 minutes until softened. Add the chorizo and cook for 1 minute, then add the red pepper, turmeric and smoked paprika, then the rice and cook for 2 minutes, stirring.

Add the chicken and half the stock. Bring to the boil over a medium-high heat, then turn the heat down to low and simmer for about 10–12 minutes, stirring occasionally, until most of the liquid has been absorbed.

Add the prawns, peas and the remaining stock, bring to the boil, then turn the heat down to low and simmer for a further 8–10 minutes until almost all the liquid has been absorbed and the chicken and prawns are cooked. Season with salt and pepper to taste, then add the parsley.

Serve the paella on its own for a simple, impressive and delicious supper.

Serves 4
Preparation time: 15 minutes, plus making the stock
Cooking time: 30 minutes

4 tbsp olive oil
30g/1oz unsalted butter
1 large onion, finely chopped
2 garlic cloves, crushed
150g/5½oz chorizo, diced
1 large red pepper, deseeded and sliced
1 tsp turmeric
1 tbsp smoked paprika
220g/7¾oz/1 cup paella or risotto rice, such as Arborio
400g/14oz chicken fillet strips, cut into chunks
600ml/21fl oz/scant 2½ cups Chicken Stock (see page 197)
200g/7oz raw tiger prawns, shell on
100g/3½oz fresh podded or frozen peas
2 tbsp chopped parsley leaves
sea salt and freshly ground black pepper

Chicken, bok choy & toasted peanut stir-fry

Stir-frys are another great way to rustle up a quick, healthy and interesting meal when you are pushed for time. Make sure your pan is hot when you add the ingredients and keep them moving around the pan all the time so they cook evenly and do not burn.

Dust the chicken strips lightly in the cornflour. Heat a wok or frying pan over a high heat. Add the sesame oil and fish sauce, then add the chicken strips and fry for 1 minute, stirring continuously.

Add the garlic, bok choy, peanuts and bean sprouts and toss together. Add the vinegar, soy sauce and stock, stir together well and bring to the boil. Cook for a further 2 minutes, still stirring, until the chicken is cooked through and the sauce has reduced and thickened. Season with salt and pepper to taste. Serve straight away and enjoy.

Serves 4
Preparation time: 10 minutes, plus making the stock
Cooking time: 10 minutes

4 skinless chicken breasts, cut into strips
1 tbsp cornflour
1 tbsp sesame oil
1 tsp Thai fish sauce
1 garlic clove, chopped
4 bok choy, halved
80g/2¾oz/½ cup peanuts
80g/2¾oz bean sprouts
1 tbsp raspberry vinegar
1 tbsp light soy sauce
150ml/5fl oz/scant ⅔ cup Chicken Stock (see page 197)
sea salt and freshly ground black pepper

Chicken with crispy noodles

A quick and easy stir-fry that makes a great lunch or supper dish, this is perfect for the busy lives we all lead – and it's healthy too. I'm also convinced that you'll love my simple, new twist of combining the chicken with crispy instead of soft noodles.

Bring a saucepan of water to the boil over a high heat. Add the egg noodles and cook for 3–4 minutes until tender. Drain well, then divide the noodles into four piles.

Heat at least 5cm/2in of the groundnut oil in a deep, heavy-based saucepan to 180°C/350°F, when a cube of bread browns in 50 seconds. Using a large, flat, round slotted spoon, lower in the first pile of noodles and fry for about 1 minute until golden, then lift back out and drain on kitchen paper. Repeat with the remaining noodles. Keep them warm until required.

Meanwhile, heat the sesame oil in a large frying pan over a medium heat. Add the garlic and chicken and fry for 2 minutes, stirring. Add the peppers and carrots and fry for a further 2–3 minutes until the peppers are just soft. Add the mirin, vinegar and soy sauce and stir well, then add the cabbage. Turn the heat up to high and stir-fry for a few minutes until all the ingredients are well blended and the chicken is cooked through.

Put the crispy noodle nests on plates, spoon the chicken into the centre with a little sauce – and it's time to eat.

Serves 4
Preparation time: 15 minutes
Cooking time: 10 minutes

300g/10½oz egg noodles
groundnut oil, for deep-frying
1 tbsp sesame oil
2 garlic cloves, finely chopped
4 skinless chicken breasts, cut into thin strips
½ red pepper, deseeded and finely diced
½ green pepper, deseeded and finely diced
2 carrots, peeled and cut into fine julienne strips
1 tsp mirin
1 tsp rice wine vinegar
4 tbsp light soy sauce
1 spring cabbage, finely sliced

Chicken macaroni cheese with crispy pancetta

I love the change of texture and added interest that you get by adding chicken to macaroni cheese, so that's what I've done with this recipe. Plus I've spiced it up with a little mustard and included some crispy pancetta for a more rounded flavour. This is the kind of classic recipe that doesn't need to be radically modernized because it is so good, just tweaked a little.

Preheat the oven to 180°C/350°F/Gas 4. Line a baking tray with baking paper and lay the strips of pancetta on top, then cover with another sheet of baking paper and top with a second baking tray to press them as they cook. Bake for 10–12 minutes until flat and crisp, then leave to cool.

Meanwhile, heat the oil in a frying pan over a medium-high heat. Season the chicken with salt and pepper, add to the pan and fry for 2 minutes on each side until lightly coloured. Very carefully add 100ml/3^1/3fl oz/scant ^{1}/2 cup water – it will sizzle and spit – turn the heat down to low, partially cover and cook for about 10 minutes until the juices run clear when the thickest part of the chicken is pierced with the tip of a sharp knife. Remove from the pan and cut into small pieces.

While the chicken is cooking, bring a large saucepan of lightly salted water to the boil, add the macaroni and return to the boil. Simmer for 10–12 minutes until just tender. Drain well, then return it to the hot pan and drizzle a little oil over the pasta to stop it sticking together.

Melt the butter in a saucepan over a medium-high heat, then add the onion and garlic and cook for 2 minutes until softened. Add the flour and cook for a further minute, stirring, then gradually add the milk, stirring continuously as the sauce starts to thicken. Stir in the mascarpone and the mustards, then three-quarters of the Cheddar cheese and keep stirring until melted. Add the chicken and season with salt and pepper to taste.

Stir the cheese sauce into the macaroni, then spoon it into an ovenproof dish. Sprinkle with the remaining Cheddar cheese and bake for 15 minutes until the cheese is melted and golden. Top with the pancetta and serve with a salad.

Serves 4
Preparation time: 20 minutes
Cooking time: 40 minutes

8 slices of pancetta
1 tbsp olive oil, plus extra for drizzling
2 skinless chicken breasts
250g/9oz macaroni
1 tsp salt
40g/1^1/2oz unsalted butter
1 onion, finely diced
1 garlic clove, finely diced
40g/1^1/2oz/^{1}/3 cup plain flour
500ml/17fl oz/2 cups milk
1 tbsp mascarpone cheese
1 tsp Dijon mustard
^{1}/2 tsp English mustard
150g/5^1/2oz mature Cheddar cheese, grated
freshly ground black pepper
1 recipe quantity Microleaf & Carrot Salad (see page 219), to serve

Chicken, leek & cream linguine

Preheat the oven to 200°C/400°F/Gas 6. Season the chicken with salt and pepper. Heat half the oil in a frying pan over a medium-high heat and fry the chicken for 2–3 minutes on each side until browned, then transfer to a roasting tin. Roast for 10–12 minutes, or until the juices run clear when the thickest part of the chicken is pierced with the tip of a sharp knife. Leave the cooked chicken to rest in a warm place.

Meanwhile, bring a saucepan of water to the boil over a high heat. Add the leeks and blanch for 30 seconds, then drain, refresh in ice-cold water, drain again and leave to one side.

Melt the butter and the remaining oil in a frying pan over a medium-low heat. Add the shallots, garlic, lemon zest and a little salt and fry for 3 minutes until softened but not browned. Turn the heat up to high, add the wine and boil for 4–5 minutes until almost all the wine has evaporated. Add the stock and boil to reduce again by two-thirds. Reduce the heat to low, add the cream and simmer for a few minutes until the sauce has slightly thickened and coats the back of a spoon.

While the sauce is cooking, bring another saucepan of salted water to the boil over a high heat. Add the linguine, return to the boil and cook for about 5 minutes, or as directed on the packet. Drain and keep warm.

Strain the sauce through a sieve into a clean saucepan, pushing the shallots with the back of a spoon to make sure all the flavour is squeezed out. Discard the shallots. Bring the cream sauce back to a simmer over a medium heat and stir in the mustard and lemon juice. Season with salt and pepper to taste.

Spoon the pasta into serving bowls and pour over the sauce. Scatter the leeks and chives over the top, then slice the chicken and put on top of the creamy pasta, Serve with a fresh, green salad.

Serves 4
Preparation time: 15 minutes, plus making the stock
Cooking time: 20 minutes

4 chicken breasts, skin on
2 tbsp olive oil
5 baby leeks, trimmed and sliced on the diagonal
2 tbsp unsalted butter
4 shallots, sliced
2 garlic cloves, skin on, crushed
2 strips of lemon zest
200ml/7fl oz/scant 1 cup dry white wine
200ml/7fl oz/scant 1 cup Chicken Stock (see page 197)
200ml/7fl oz/scant 1 cup double cream
300g/10½oz linguine
1 tbsp wholegrain mustard
a small squeeze of lemon juice
1 tbsp very finely chopped chives
sea salt and freshly ground black pepper
1 recipe quantity Green Salad (see page 219), to serve

Crispy chicken & potato crust

This unusul twist on the classic combination of chicken and chips is a real crowd pleaser, offering a modern interpretation of this great pairing – succulent meat and crunchy, golden potatoes. It makes for a filling yet impressive dish for any occasion. Cutting the chicken into strips makes it mega child-friendly, but you can cook the chicken breasts whole if you prefer, then slice them on the diagonal to serve, giving the dish a slightly more grown-up look. It also goes really well with buttered carrots or kale.

Preheat the oven to 160°C/315°F/Gas 2½. Season the chicken breasts with salt and pepper. Put the grated potatoes on a shallow plate and press with kitchen paper to soak up any excess moisture. Whisk the eggs in a second shallow plate. Put the flour on a third shallow plate and season with salt and pepper. Toss the potatoes in the flour, shaking off any excess. Press the chicken strips into the potato mixture, shaping it around and pressing gently to seal the chicken within the grated potato casing.

Heat the oil and butter in a frying pan over a medium-high heat. Add the potato-wrapped chicken a few pieces at a time and cook for about 12 minutes until golden brown on all sides and cooked through. Keep the cooked chicken warm in the oven while you cook the remainder.

Serve the chicken with mushy peas.

Serves 4
Preparation time: 25 minutes
Cooking time: 30 minutes

4 skinless chicken breasts, cut into thick
  strips
6–8 large floury potatoes, such as Maris
  Piper, peeled and grated but not rinsed
1 egg, beaten
2 tbsp plain flour
2–3 tbsp olive oil
30g/1oz unsalted butter
sea salt and freshly ground black pepper
mushy peas, to serve

Chive chicken with creamed cabbage

A chicken supreme is the breast of the chicken with the wing bone attached. If you joint your own chickens (see pages 18–19), they are easy to prepare. Otherwise, just ask the butcher to prepare them for you. They are usually happy to do so.

Preheat the oven to 190°C/375°F/Gas 5 and season the chicken with salt and pepper. Heat half the oil in a large, heavy-based frying pan over a high heat, then add the chicken and fry for about 2 minutes on each side until well browned and the meat has started to caramelize.

Transfer the chicken to a roasting tin and roast for 10–12 minutes until the juices run clear when the thickest part of the chicken is pierced with the tip of a sharp knife.

Meanwhile, heat the remaining oil in a large saucepan over a medium-high heat. Add the bacon and fry for 3–4 minutes until crisp and golden brown. Add the cabbage and butter and cook for a further 3–4 minutes, stirring, until the cabbage starts to soften. Add the wine and cream and bring to the boil.

Reduce the heat to low and simmer for 5–6 minutes, stirring occasionally, until the mixture has reduced to a thick sauce. Stir in the chives. Spoon the sauce over the chicken and serve with mashed potatoes.

Serves 4
Preparation time: 10 minutes
Cooking time: 20 minutes

4 chicken supremes, skin on
2 tbsp groundnut oil
150g/5^{1}/2oz smoked bacon lardons
300g/10^{1}/2oz cabbage, chopped
55g/2oz unsalted butter
80ml/2^{1}/2fl oz/^{1}/3 cup white wine
200ml/7fl oz/scant 1 cup double cream
2 tbsp chopped chives
sea salt and freshly ground black pepper
1 recipe quantity Creamy Mashed Potatoes
   (see page 212), to serve

Chicken fricassée

Chicken fricassée is a very simple and delicate dish made up of small pieces of meat cooked in a light white sauce. It is important to use a good-quality chicken stock so make your own or buy from the chill cabinet, if you can, rather than using a stock cube.

Melt half the butter in a frying pan over a low heat. Add the mushrooms and cook for 5 minutes until just tender, then remove from the pan.

Add the remaining butter to the pan. Season the chicken with salt and pepper and add to the pan. Cook for a few minutes on each side until sealed but without colouring the chicken.

Add the flour and cook for 2 minutes, stirring continuously, then turn up the heat to medium and gradually add the stock, still stirring. Bring to the boil, then turn the heat down to low and simmer for about 15 minutes until the chicken juices run clear when the thickest part of the chicken is pierced with the tip of a sharp knife.

Whisk together the egg yolk and cream with a pinch of salt in a bowl or jug, then whisk in a ladleful of the hot stock. Stir the mixture into the frying pan and season with a little salt and pepper. Add the cooked mushrooms and the parsley and simmer for a further 5 minutes until piping hot and well blended.

Serve the chicken with buttered carrots.

Serves 4
Preparation time: 20 minutes,
  plus making the stock
Cooking time: 35 minutes

50g/1¾oz unsalted butter
100g/3½oz button mushrooms
12 skinless boneless chicken thighs,
  cut into chunks
35g/1¼oz/scant ⅓ cup plain flour
500ml/17fl oz/2 cups Chicken Stock
  (see page 197)
1 egg yolk
3 tbsp double cream
2 tbsp chopped parsley leaves
sea salt and freshly ground black pepper
1 recipe quantity Buttered Carrots (see
  page 216), to serve

Spice-rubbed, roasted half chicken with smoky bacon chips

Roast chicken is healthy, full of protein and a classic dish but it's hardly something new, so here is my modern take on roast chicken, adding a spicy rub that gives your taste buds a kick and makes sure you and yours sit up and take notice. Plus, these are no ordinary chips as they are sprinkled with my smoky bacon crumb – different and delicious. You can easily keep the rub in an airtight container for a few days, so make it in advance to speed up an after-work meal.

Start soaking, then cooking the chips, following steps 1 and 2 on page 213.

Meanwhile, mix together all the spice rub ingredients. Put the half chickens in a roasting tin and rub the mix all over. Cover and leave to marinate in the fridge for 20 minutes.

To make the smoky bacon mix, preheat the grill to high, then grill the pancetta for about 5 minutes until very crisp. Drain well on kitchen paper, then leave to cool. Put in a small blender with the remaining smoky bacon mix ingredients and blitz to a fine powder.

Heat the oil in a griddle pan over a high heat, add the chicken halves in batches and cook for 2–3 minutes on each side until coloured, then transfer to a roasting tin and roast for 8–10 minutes until the juices run clear when the thickest part of the chicken is pierced with the tip of a sharp knife.

Meanwhile, finish cooking the chips, following step 3 on page 213.

Season the chips with a little salt, then sprinkle the smoky bacon crumb generously over the chips. Serve the chicken with the smoky bacon chips and coleslaw.

Serves 4
Preparation time: 30 minutes, plus 20 minutes marinating
Cooking time: 30 minutes

1 recipe quantity Chips (see page 213)
1 tbsp olive oil
4 half chickens
sea salt and freshly ground black pepper
1 recipe quantity Celeriac & Carrot Coleslaw (see page 218), to serve

FOR THE SPICE RUB
2 tbsp smoked paprika
1 tbsp smoked sea salt, finely ground
1 tbsp sugar
1 tbsp mustard powder
2 tsp chilli powder
1 tbsp ground cumin
1 tbsp ground black pepper
1 tbsp granulated garlic
1 tbsp cayenne pepper

FOR THE SMOKY BACON MIX
8 strips of pancetta, chopped
$\frac{1}{2}$ tsp cayenne pepper
2 tsp smoked paprika
2 tsp dark soft brown sugar

Homemade crumpets with chicken & chive-scrambled eggs

Homemade crumpets are something a little bit special – I often used to eat them as a child with lots of butter. Most people wouldn't think of making them, but they are actually quite easy to make yourself – and even easier if you buy some crumpet rings from any cookshop, although if you don't have any, just use a large round pastry cutter. Crumpets go really well with soft scrambled egg and fresh chives, making this a perfect little recipe for breakfast or brunch.

Bring the milk just to lukewarm in a saucepan over a medium heat. Whisk in the yeast until dissolved. Mix together the flour, sugar and salt in a bowl, then gradually add the milk and yeast mixture, stirring continuously. Stir in 125ml/4fl oz/½ cup lukewarm water and whisk together until completely combined. Cover with cling film and leave to rise in a warm place for 1½ hours.

Stir the baking powder and half the oil into the batter mix. Heat the remaining oil in a non-stick frying pan over a medium-high heat and use a piece of kitchen paper to grease the pan. Also grease with oil or cold water the inside of as many crumpet rings as will fit in the pan, then put the rings in the pan. Pour some of the batter mix into each ring, filling them three-quarters full, and cook for 2 minutes, then turn the heat down to low and cook for a further 3 minutes until the tops are drying out and have a few holes. Flip the crumpets over, using a palette knife, and cook for a further 1–2 minutes until firm. Remove from the pan and leave on a wire rack while you cook the remaining crumpets.

Meanwhile, to make the scrambled eggs, whisk together the eggs and chives in a saucepan over a medium heat. Add the shredded chicken and season with salt and pepper. Cook for 4–5 minutes, stirring every 30–60 seconds to stop the eggs overcooking. Stir in the butter and serve immediately with the warm crumpets.

Serves 4
Preparation time: 15 minutes, plus 1½ hours rising
Cooking time: 15 minutes

FOR THE CRUMPETS
170ml/5½fl oz/⅔ cup milk
10g/¼oz/1 tbsp fresh yeast or 1½ tsp dried yeast
225g/8oz/heaped 1¾ cups plain flour
2 tsp caster sugar
1 tsp salt
2 tsp baking powder
2 tbsp olive oil

FOR THE CHIVE-SCRAMBLED EGGS
10 eggs, beaten
3 tbsp chopped chives
1 smoked chicken breast (see page 23), shredded
2 tbsp unsalted butter
sea salt and freshly ground black pepper

Chicken huevos rancheros

Bring a bit of Mexican flavour into your kitchen with this tasty dish of refried beans with all the trimmings. If you like your food spicy, you can increase the amount of chilli you add to the dish. If you are short of time, simply serve with a shop-bought guacamole.

Heat the butter and half the oil in a frying pan over a medium heat, add the onion and garlic and fry for 3–4 minutes until soft.

Add the chorizo, bacon and chicken and fry, stirring, for 5 minutes until coloured and just cooked through. Add the refried beans and tomatoes. Stir in the chilli, jalapeño pepper and coriander and season with salt and pepper to taste. Cook for a further 10 minutes until all the ingredients are hot and well blended.

Meanwhile, in a separate frying pan, heat the remaining oil and fry the eggs until the yolks are just cooked. Slide the eggs on top of the chicken mixture and sprinkle with the grated cheese. Serve the huevos rancheros hot with the guacamole.

Serves 4
Preparation time: 15 minutes
Cooking time: 20 minutes

1 tbsp butter
2 tbsp olive oil
1 onion, finely diced
1 garlic clove, chopped
60g/2¼oz chorizo, chopped
1 thick smoked bacon rasher, diced
150g/5½oz minced chicken
250g/9oz refried beans
200g/7oz/¾ cup tinned chopped tomatoes
½ red chilli, deseeded and chopped
1 jalapeño pepper, deseeded and chopped
4 tbsp chopped coriander leaves
4 large eggs
3 tbsp grated Cheddar cheese
sea salt and freshly ground black pepper
1 recipe quantity Guacamole
  (see page 201), to serve

Chicken Niçoise with caper & roasted tomato dressing

I began with a classic Niçoise salad but this one has my own little twists – a steamed chicken breast to keep it nice and healthy, a tomato dressing made with capers to give it definition, and a delicious sprinkling of olive crumb on the top.

Preheat the oven to 140°C/275°F/Gas 1. Reserve a few olives and bake the remainder for 30 minutes until dried out, then leave to cool and chop finely.

Meanwhile, put a large saucepan of water on to simmer, with a steamer insert on top. Season the chicken with salt and pepper, then put it into the steamer, cover and cook for 20–25 minutes until the juices run clear when the thickest part of the chicken is pierced with the tip of a sharp knife.

At the same time, put the potatoes in a saucepan of cold water and bring to the boil over a high heat, then turn the heat down to low and simmer for 10 minutes until tender, then drain. Bring a small saucepan of water to the boil over a high heat, add the green beans and cook for 2 minutes. Drain, then run the beans under ice-cold water to stop them from cooking further. Drain, then leave to one side.

Meanwhile, bring a saucepan of water to the boil over a high heat. Gently lower the eggs into the water, then boil for 6½ minutes. Lift the eggs out of the water, using a slotted spoon, place in a bowl of ice-cold water to stop them from cooking further and leave to cool for 5 minutes. Peel in the water, to stop them from breaking, then drain.

Grind the peppercorns and salt in a spice grinder or pestle and mortar, then tip into a shallow bowl. Roll the peeled egg in the mixture. Whisk together the dressing ingredients in a bowl, then season with salt and pepper.

Slice the chicken and halve the eggs, then put on top of the beans, potatoes and olive halves. Drizzle with the tomato dressing and finish with a few pinches of olive crumb.

Serves 4
Preparation time: 20 minutes, plus making the slow-roasted tomatoes
Cooking time: 30 minutes

100g/3½oz/scant ¾ cup pitted black or green olives, halved
4 skinless chicken breasts
400g/14oz baby new potatoes
150g/5½oz fine green beans
4 eggs
2 tbsp black peppercorns
1 tsp sea salt

FOR THE CAPER & ROASTED TOMATO DRESSING
6 tbsp Slow-Roasted Tomatoes (see page 218)
2 tbsp drained capers
2 tbsp red wine vinegar or raspberry vinegar
6 tbsp olive oil

Chicken, lemongrass & thyme Scotch eggs with mustard mayonnaise

I mastered this dish when I was running a pub, but these are no ordinary Scotch eggs because I've brought in the new perspective of Far Eastern flavours. The bright and runny yolks from my mother-in-law's free-range eggs are encased in moist, flavoursome meat and a crisp crumb.

Preheat the oven to 200°C/400°F/Gas 6. Bring a saucepan of water to the boil over a high heat. Gently lower the eggs into the water, then boil for 6½ minutes. Lift the eggs out, using a slotted spoon, put in a bowl of ice-cold water to stop them cooking further and leave for 5 minutes. Peel them in the water, to stop them from breaking, then drain.

While the eggs are cooling, mix together the meat coating ingredients, seasoning with plenty of salt and pepper. Prepare the ingredients for the breadcrumb coating by putting the flour and breadcrumbs in two separate shallow bowls. In a third bowl, whisk together the eggs and milk and season with a pinch of salt to make an egg wash.

Roll the hard-boiled eggs in the flour. Dust your hands with a little more flour and pat out one-quarter of the chicken mixture into a flat oval on your hand. Put a boiled egg in the centre and gently wrap the meat around the egg so that it is evenly covered, pinching the edges together to seal. Roll the egg in the egg wash, shaking off any excess, roll in the breadcrumbs, then roll in egg wash and breadcrumbs again. Repeat with the remaining eggs.

Heat the oil in a deep, heavy-based saucepan to 170°C/ 325°F, when a cube of bread browns in 60 seconds. Gently lower the eggs into the oil, using a slotted spoon, and cook for 8–10 minutes, turning occasionally, until the breadcrumbs are a dark golden brown. Remove from the oil and drain on kitchen paper for 2–3 minutes, then transfer to the oven for 10 minutes to ensure that the chicken is cooked through but the outside is not too brown. Mix the mustard into the mayonnaise. Halve the eggs and serve with the flavoured mayonnaise and a fresh salad.

Serves 4
Preparation time: 30 minutes, plus making the mayonnaise
Cooking time: 25 minutes

4 large eggs
sunflower oil, for deep-frying
1 tsp Dijon mustard
150ml/5fl oz/scant ⅔ cup Mayonnaise (see page 202)
1 recipe quantity Green Salad (see page 219), to serve

FOR THE CHICKEN & THYME COATING
400g/14oz minced chicken
1 lemongrass stalk, finely chopped
leaves from 2 thyme sprigs, finely chopped
grated zest and juice of 1 lemon
sea salt and freshly ground black pepper

FOR THE BREADCRUMB COATING
4 tbsp plain flour
100g/3½oz/1 cup panko breadcrumbs or fine dried breadcrumbs
4 eggs
125ml/4fl oz/½ cup milk

Chicken & spring onion patties with red onion, tomato & coriander salad

A light and healthy recipe, these neat little patties make a lovely simple snack that can be served as a starter, canapé or even a light lunch. Team them with any fresh salad ingredients to ring the changes, or add a few chips or buttered new potatoes to make a more substantial meal.

Mix together all the ingredients for the patties, cover with cling film and chill in the fridge for 30 minutes.

Shape the chicken mixture into 8 small burgers. Heat the frying oils in a frying pan until shimmering, then add the patties and fry for 2 minutes on each side until cooked through and golden. Drain on kitchen paper.

Meanwhile, mix together the salad ingredients, adding a little dressing to taste. Serve the patties with the fresh onion, tomato and herb salad.

Serves 4
Preparation time: 15 minutes, plus 30 minutes chilling, and making the dressing
Cooking time: 5 minutes

FOR THE CHICKEN & SPRING ONION PATTIES
400g/14oz minced chicken
4 spring onions, finely diced
1 tbsp light soy sauce
2 tbsp chopped coriander leaves
1 tbsp sesame oil
1 garlic clove, finely chopped
1 tsp Worcestershire sauce
2 tbsp peeled and grated root ginger
2 tbsp sesame seeds
1 red chilli, deseeded and finely chopped

2 tbsp olive oil, for frying
1 tsp sesame oil, for frying

FOR THE ONION, TOMATO & CORIANDER SALAD
2 red onions, finely sliced
2 tbsp chopped coriander leaves
3 vine tomatoes, finely diced
sea salt and freshly ground black pepper
a drizzle of Bean House Salad Dressing (see page 203)

Curried chicken pasties with mango chutney

I love a hot pasty with flaky, well-cooked pastry, a flavoursome filling and, of course, you always need a sauce or chutney. These little morsels of spicy chicken with mango chutney are a slice of heaven. The recipe makes eight small pasties but you could make four large ones, if you prefer.

To make the pastry, put the flour, salt and sugar in a bowl, then rub in the butter, using your fingertips, until the mixture resembles coarse breadcrumbs. Stir in 1 egg and about 1 tablespoon water, if necessary, a drop at a time, to bind the ingredients together. Roll into a ball, wrap in cling film and chill in the fridge while you make the filling.

Melt the butter in a frying pan over a medium heat. Add the onion and curry paste and fry for about 3 minutes until the onions are soft but not brown. Add the carrot and cook for 2 minutes. Toss the chicken with the cornflour to coat, then add to the pan and fry for a further 2–3 minutes, stirring, until the chicken is just coloured.

Add the sweetcorn and stock, stirring until it comes to the boil. Turn the heat down to low and cook for a further 2–3 minutes until the chicken is cooked through. Add the cream and cook for a further few minutes until the sauce thickens. Season with salt and pepper to taste, then remove from the heat and leave to one side to cool.

Preheat the oven to 200°C/400°F/Gas 6 and grease a baking tray. Roll out the pastry on a lightly floured work surface and cut out either 4 large or 8 small equal-sized circles. Spoon the filling in the centre of the pastry rounds. Mix the remaining egg with 1 tablespoon water to make an egg wash and brush around the edges of the pastry, then bring both sides to meet at the top to contain the chicken mix. Crimp the top to seal the pasties by pushing the pastry between the index finger of one hand against the index finger and thumb of the other hand. Put on the prepared baking tray and bake for 8–10 minutes, then brush with the remaining egg wash and return to the oven for a further 8–10 minutes until golden.

Serve the pasties with mango chutney and a fresh salad.

Serves 4
Preparation time: 30 minutes, plus making the curry paste and stock
Cooking time: 35 minutes

FOR THE PASTRY
250g/9oz/2 cups plain flour, plus extra for dusting
a pinch of salt
½ tsp caster sugar
125g/4½oz cold unsalted butter, diced
2 eggs

FOR THE CURRIED CHICKEN FILLING
50g/1¾oz unsalted butter, plus extra for greasing
1 onion, finely diced
1 tbsp Curry Paste (see page 204)
1 carrot, peeled and finely diced
2 skinless chicken breasts, cubed
1 tsp cornflour
200g/7oz/1 cup drained tinned sweetcorn kernels
200ml/7fl oz/scant 1 cup Chicken Stock (see page 197)
100ml/3½fl oz/scant ½ cup double cream
sea salt and freshly ground black pepper

4 tbsp Mango Chutney (see page 206)
1 recipe quantity Herb Salad (see page 219)

Chicken & sesame prawn toasts

I've always been a fan of sesame prawn toast, especially when served with homemade sweet and sour chilli sauce like the one I serve with my Vietnamese-style wraps (see page 161). But the addition of the chicken just lifts it to another level, as the chicken and prawn work really well together. It makes a great snack or a delicious starter.

Preheat the oven to 200°C/400°F/Gas 6. Put the prawns, chicken, ginger, soy sauce, spring onions, sesame oil and a pinch of salt in a blender and blitz to a paste. Spoon the paste onto the slices of baguette to make a nice mound in the centre, leaving a small space around the edge. Put the baguette slices on a plate and sprinkle liberally with the sesame seeds, covering the prawn paste.

Heat the oil in a large frying pan over a medium heat, add the slices, paste-side down, and fry for 2–3 minutes until golden brown, then flip over and fry the other sides for a further 2 minutes.

Transfer to a baking tray and roast for 2–3 minutes to dry out. Leave to cool before serving.

Serves 4
Preparation time: 15 minutes
Cooking time: 10 minutes

150g/5½oz raw peeled tiger prawns
1 skinless boneless chicken thigh
1 tbsp peeled and finely chopped root
   ginger
1 tbsp soy sauce
1 tbsp chopped spring onions
1 tsp sesame oil
a pinch of salt
12 slices of baguette, ideally a few
   days old and slightly dry
4 tbsp sesame seeds
150ml/5fl oz/scant ⅔ cup groundnut oil
sea salt

Sticky barbecued chicken wings

There are times when you don't really want a big meal, but prefer to graze on smaller, easy-to-eat items, and these barbecued wings definitely fit the bill. For best results, make your own coleslaw, if you have the time, then you know it is fresh and crunchy.

Mix together all the marinade ingredients in a bowl until well blended. Stir in the chicken wings, making sure they are well coated. Cover with cling film and leave to marinate in the fridge for 2–3 hours or ideally overnight.

Preheat the oven to 200°C/400°F/Gas 6. Spread the chicken wings evenly in a large roasting tin, pouring any excess marinade over the top. Roast for 20–30 minutes until the wings are cooked through and the marinade has caramelized so it is nice and sticky. Serve warm on their own or with coleslaw.

Serves 4
Preparation time: 15 minutes, plus at least 2 hours marinating
Cooking time: 30 minutes

12 chicken wings, skin on
1 recipe quantity Celeriac & Carrot Coleslaw (see page 218), to serve

FOR THE STICKY BARBECUE MARINADE
3 tbsp tomato ketchup
1½ tbsp soy sauce
1½ tsp smoked paprika
1 tsp smoked salt or sea salt
1½ tbsp clear honey
2 garlic cloves, finely chopped
3cm/1¼in piece of root ginger, peeled and finely chopped
2 tbsp groundnut oil

Chicken tacos with tomato salsa & guacamole

Mexican food has a great balance of fresh, spicy and fragrant flavours with lots of coriander in most recipes. I really like tacos and find them a quick and easy meal to make for friends that is great for keeping everything nice and relaxed. Since you can make most of this recipe in advance, you've got more time to enjoy with your friends – and a bottle or two of Mexican lager.

Heat the oil in a large saucepan over a medium heat. Add the garlic, onion and red pepper and fry for 2–3 minutes until just soft. Add the chicken and cook for 3–4 minutes, stirring, until the chicken is just starting to colour. Add the dry spices and mix everything together well, then add the chicken stock and bring to the boil. Turn the heat down to low, cover and simmer for 15–20 minutes, stirring every 5 minutes, until the liquid has evaporated and the chicken is browned and cooked through.

While the chicken is cooking, make the tomato salsa and the guacamole and preheat the oven to 180°C/350°F/Gas 4. Warm the tacos in the oven for 2–3 minutes so they are all ready when your chicken is cooked.

Fill the tacos with the chicken mixture and top with spoonfuls of tomato salsa and guacamole. Sprinkle with grated cheese and serve with the lime wedges.

Serves 4
Preparation time: 10 minutes, plus making the stock, salsa and guacamole
Cooking time: 30 minutes

1 tbsp olive oil
2 garlic cloves, finely chopped
1 onion, finely diced
1 red pepper, deseeded and finely chopped
500g/1lb 2oz minced chicken
1 tsp smoked paprika
½ tsp chilli powder
½ tsp ground cumin
1 tsp ground coriander
200ml/7fl oz/scant 1 cup Chicken Stock (see page 197)
1 recipe quantity Tomato Salsa (see page 201)
1 recipe quantity Guacamole (see page 201)
16 taco shells
100g/3½oz mature Cheddar cheese, grated
1 lime, cut into wedges

Hazelnut, chicken & tarragon empanadas

Empanadas are small, savoury pasties, common in Spain and Portugal. They come with all different fillings and there are even empanada festivals, championing the regional specialities. I've chosen to partner the chicken with the strong, sharp flavour of tarragon with soft mushrooms and toasted hazelnuts – or cobnuts as I call them – for that extra bit of texture, and I've wrapped that delicious combination in a crisp short pastry.

Melt the butter in a large saucepan over a medium heat. Add the onion and garlic and fry for 3–4 minutes until softened. Add the mushrooms and cook for 2 minutes, then add the minced chicken and cook for about 5 minutes, stirring, until just browned.

Add the stock, then the tarragon and simmer for 5 minutes to reduce the liquid, then add the cream and simmer gently for a further 5 minutes.

Add the spinach and hazelnuts, season with salt and pepper to taste, and stir everything together well. Transfer to a bowl and leave to cool slightly, then cover with cling film and chill in the fridge for about 30 minutes until the mixture firms up slightly.

Preheat the oven to 200°C/400°F/Gas 6 and line a baking sheet with baking paper. Divide the pastry into 8 equal pieces and roll out one piece at a time on a lightly floured work surface into a circle about 3mm/1/8in thick. Spoon one-eighth of the cold meat mixture into the centre. Brush the edges with a little cold water, then fold half of the dough over the top and seal the edges together by pressing with the tines of a fork. Repeat the process to make 8 empanadas.

Place the sealed empanadas on the prepared baking tray. Beat the egg with 1 tablespoon water and brush over the empanadas, then bake for 10 minutes until golden brown.

Serve hot or cold with a fresh salad.

Serves 4
Preparation time: 30 minutes, plus 30 minutes chilling, and making the stock and pastry
Cooking time: 30 minutes

40g/1½oz unsalted butter
1 onion, finely sliced
1 garlic clove, diced
100g/3½oz chestnut mushrooms, quartered
250g/9oz minced chicken
100ml/3½fl oz/scant ½ cup Chicken Stock (see page 197)
1 tbsp chopped tarragon leaves
100ml/3½fl oz/scant ½ cup double cream
50g/1¾oz chopped spinach leaves
150g/5½oz/heaped 1 cup toasted hazelnuts, roughly chopped
1 recipe quantity Shortcrust Pastry (see page 208)
a little flour, for dusting
1 egg
sea salt and freshly ground black pepper
1 recipe quantity Green Salad (see page 219) or a mixed salad, to serve

Chicken corn dogs

Corn dogs are an all-American classic street food, traditionally made with a frankfurter dipped in a batter and deep-fried. Here I've made them with chicken because the tasty sausages work so well with the crispy coating. Why not try them for an evening barbecue, as they will be sure to be popular with the whole family.

Put eight wooden skewers in a bowl of cold water to soak for 1 hour. Put all the sauce ingredients in a saucepan over a high heat and bring to the boil. Turn the heat down to low, cover the pan and simmer for about 30 minutes until the sauce is rich and thick, stirring occasionally and adding a little more water if the sauce becomes too dry. Leave it chunky or purée in a blender for a smooth sauce.

Meanwhile, mix together the cornmeal, flour, sugar, nutmeg and baking powder, add the eggs and milk and whisk together to form thick batter. Pour the batter into a straight pint glass.

Heat the oil in a deep, heavy-based saucepan to 180°C/350°F, when a cube of day-old bread will brown in 40 seconds. Thread the skewers lengthways through the sausages.

Dip the first sausage into the glass with the batter until coated, then slowly lift it out and submerge it in the hot oil, turning occasionally for 3–4 minutes until browned. Remove from the oil, drain on kitchen paper for 1 minute, then keep them warm while you cook the remaining corn dogs. Serve with the barbecue sauce.

Serves 4
Preparation time: 15 minutes,
  plus making the sausages
Cooking time: 20 minutes

150g/5½oz/1 cup cornmeal or polenta
125g/4½oz/1 cup self-raising flour
30g/1oz caster sugar
a small pinch of grated nutmeg
2 tsp baking powder
1 egg
230ml/7¾fl oz/scant 1 cup semi-
  skimmed milk
groundnut oil, for deep-frying
8 cooked Chicken & Pancetta Sausages
  (see page 120)
sea salt and freshly ground black pepper

FOR THE BARBECUE SAUCE
400g/14oz/scant 1⅔ cups tinned chopped
  tomatoes
1 tsp smoked paprika
1 tbsp fresh apple juice
2 tbsp balsamic vinegar
1 tbsp Worcestershire sauce
80g/2¾oz/scant ½ cup dark soft brown
  sugar
1 tbsp tomato ketchup
a few drops of Tabasco sauce

Pulled chicken baps with barbecue sauce

There's something a bit special about pulled meat and barbecue sauce, and the combination works well with shredded chicken and my spicy sauce. A perfect snack for when friends drop by unannounced, you can make the sauce in advance and keep it in a sterilized airtight container in the fridge for up to two weeks.

Heat the oil in a non-stick saucepan over a medium heat. Add the onion and garlic and fry for 2–3 minutes until softened. Add all the remaining ingredients, except the bread, bring to the boil, then cover with a lid, turn down the heat to low and leave to simmer for 1 hour until the chicken is cooked through and the sauce is thick, stirring occasionally. If it gets a bit dry, add a further 3–4 tablespoons water.

Lift out the chicken from the sauce and shred the meat, using two forks. Blitz the sauce in a blender until smooth, then pass through a sieve.

To assemble the baps, mix together some chicken and sauce and pile into the baps. Serve with chips and salad, if you like.

Serves 4
Preparation time: 20 minutes
Cooking time: 1 hour 5 minutes

1 tbsp olive oil
1 onion, finely chopped
2 garlic cloves, finely chopped
2 skinless chicken breasts, sliced in half horizontally
2 skinless boneless chicken thighs
400g/14oz/scant 1²/3 cups tinned chopped tomatoes, puréed
1 tsp smoked paprika
1 tbsp fresh apple juice
2 tbsp balsamic vinegar
1 tbsp Worcestershire sauce
80g/2³/4oz/scant ½ cup dark soft brown sugar
1 tbsp tomato ketchup
a few drops of Tabasco sauce
4 white or brown baps, halved
sea salt and freshly ground black pepper
1 recipe quantity Chips (see page 213), to serve
a mixed salad (optional), to serve

Chicken, cranberry & Stilton pie

Mix together the flour, salt and pepper in a bowl and make a well in the centre. Melt the lard and butter in a saucepan with 150ml/5fl oz/scant ⅔ cup water over a low heat, then pour into the flour. Add the egg yolk and use your hands to mix to a dough. Cover with a clean tea towel and leave to cool for 5 minutes, then cover with cling film and leave for 20 minutes until cool enough to work.

Put the chicken in a saucepan and cover with water. Bring to the boil over a medium heat, then turn the heat down to low, cover with a lid and cook for 12 minutes until the juices run clear when the thickest part of the chicken is pierced with the tip of a sharp knife. Drain and leave to dry.

Preheat the oven to 220°C/425°F/Gas 7. Grease a 16cm/6¼in springform cake tin and put a baking sheet in the oven to heat up. Mix together the chicken, bacon, cranberries, Stilton, thyme and parsley and season with salt and pepper to taste.

Roll out the pastry on a lightly floured work surface to a 20cm/8in circle, then use it to line the prepared tin and overhang the edge. Fill with the meat mixture. Trim the excess pastry, roll it into a ball, then roll it out for the top. Brush the edge of the base with water and seal the lid on top by crimping the pastry edges together with a fork. Make a small hole in the centre. Mix the egg and milk and brush it over the top. Roll and cut the trimmings to decorate the top, then brush again.

Put the pie on the hot baking sheet and bake for about 20 minutes, then turn the oven down to 160°C/315°F/Gas 2½ and bake for a further 1½ hours until golden brown. Cover with kitchen foil if it gets too dark.

Soak the gelatine in cold water for 5 minutes until soft, then drain. Bring the stock to just below a simmer in a saucepan, then remove from the heat and whisk in the gelatine. Slowly pour the hot stock into the hole in the pie, stopping when it reaches the top. Leave to cool, then chill in the fridge for 2 hours. Serve with spiced apple chutney.

Serves 8
Preparation time: 30 minutes, plus cooling, 2 hours chilling, and making the stock
Cooking time: 2 hours 10 minutes

FOR THE PASTRY
450g/1lb/heaped 3½ cups plain flour, plus extra for dusting
2 tsp fine sea salt
1 tbsp freshly ground black pepper
100g/3½oz lard or vegetable fat
50g/1¾oz unsalted butter, plus extra for greasing
1 egg yolk
1 egg, lightly beaten
1 tsp milk

FOR THE CHICKEN, CRANBERRY & STILTON FILLING
2 skinless chicken breasts, cut in half horizontally
300g/10½oz skinless boneless chicken thighs, cut into 1–2cm/½–¾in pieces
1 cooked smoked back bacon rasher, finely chopped
200g/7oz/heaped 1¾ cups cranberries, defrosted if frozen
60g/2¼oz Stilton cheese, crumbled
1 tbsp chopped thyme leaves
1 tbsp chopped parsley leaves
2 sheets of gelatine
200ml/7fl oz/scant 1 cup Chicken Stock (see page 197)
sea salt and freshly ground black pepper

Spiced Apple Chutney (see page 206), to serve

Chicken, leek & ham hock pie in tarragon pastry

Growing up in pubs was great – especially since Mum always had a pie on the menu. I've given this chicken and leek pie my little twist by adding some ham hock and making it with tarragon puff pastry. You can't go wrong with a great pie to impress your friends and family.

Roll out the pastry on a lightly floured work surface, sprinkle with ½ tablespoon of the tarragon and roll it in before folding. Repeat on the following turns until all the tarragon is added to the pastry. Chill as directed.

While the pastry is chilling, heat the oil in a frying pan over a medium heat. Add the chicken and cook for 2–3 minutes on each side until just cooked. Remove from the pan and leave to one side. Wipe the pan clean, then return it to a medium heat. Add the butter, then the garlic and leeks and fry for 2–4 minutes until softened.

Sprinkle over the flour, then gradually begin to add the stock, whisking continuously so it doesn't form lumps, until you have added all the stock and the liquid has thickened slightly. It should take 4–5 minutes. Stir in the cream, then the chicken, ham and tarragon. Season with salt and pepper to taste. Remove from the heat and leave to cool slightly.

Preheat the oven to 200°C/400°F/Gas 6 and grease a 24cm/9½in pie dish with butter. Roll out the pastry to twice the size of the pie dish, then use half to line the base, trimming the edges so the pastry just sits on the rim of the dish. Spoon in the filling. Brush the edge of the pastry with a little water, then put the remaining pastry on top. Trim the edges and crimp the top and bottom together to seal the pie by pressing with the tines of a fork.

Cut a small hole in the top of the pastry to allow the steam escape. Beat the egg with 1 tablespoon water to make an egg wash, then brush it over the top of the pie. Bake for 30–40 minutes until the pastry is a lovely golden brown. Serve with buttered new potatoes and seasonal vegetables.

Serves 4
Preparation time: 30 minutes, plus at least 30 minutes chilling, and making the pastry and stock
Cooking time: 50 minutes

FOR THE PASTRY
2 recipe quantities Rough Puff Pastry (see page 208), prepared to the first chilling
a little flour, for dusting
4 tbsp chopped tarragon leaves
1 egg

FOR THE CHICKEN, LEEK & HAM FILLING
1 tbsp olive oil
6 skinless boneless chicken thighs, cut into 2cm/¾in pieces
50g/1¾oz unsalted butter, plus extra for greasing
2 garlic cloves, finely chopped
2 leeks, trimmed and finely sliced
50g/1¾oz/scant ½ cup plain flour
450ml/16fl oz/scant 2 cups Chicken Stock (see page 197)
150ml/5fl oz/scant ⅔ cup double cream
150g/5½oz cooked ham hock, shredded
1 tbsp chopped tarragon leaves
sea salt and freshly ground black pepper

boiled and buttered new potatoes and seasonal vegetables, to serve

Chicken quiche lorraine

With the delicate balance of crisp pastry and soft egg filling, quiche makes a great light lunch. But please, no soggy bottoms – bake the case blind before filling, then serve it hot or cold. You can even freeze it. Pour any leftover filling into buttered ramekins and cook for half the time.

Sift the flour into a bowl, then rub in the butter with your fingertips until the mixture resembles breadcrumbs. Make a well in the centre, add 1 egg and bring the mix together with your hands, adding 1 tablespoon water, if needed. Roll out on a lightly floured work surface until smooth. Wrap in cling film and chill in the fridge for 10 minutes.

Heat the oil in a frying pan over a medium-high heat. Add the chicken and stir-fry for 3–4 minutes until cooked through. Remove from the pan and leave to one side.

Preheat the oven to 180°C/350°F/Gas 4, put a baking tray in the oven to heat up and grease a 20cm/8in loose-bottomed flan tin. Roll out the pastry on a lightly floured work surface to 8mm/⅜in thick and use to line the prepared flan tin. Prick the base with a fork to stop the pastry from rising. Line with a double layer of cling film, then fill with dry rice. Put on the hot baking tray and bake for 12 minutes, then remove the cling film and rice.

Whisk together the remaining egg and the milk to make an egg wash and brush over the pastry, then return it to the oven for 10 minutes until golden. Leave to one side for a few minutes to cool, then chill in the fridge for 15 minutes.

To make the filling, melt the butter in a saucepan over a medium heat, add the onion and bacon and fry for 5 minutes until golden. Spoon into the pastry case, top with the chicken and sprinkle with the cheese. Whisk together the cream, milk and eggs, and season with a little salt and pepper. Pour in enough mixture to fill the pastry case.

Bake for 15–20 minutes until the filling is golden and set. If the pastry starts to go too dark, turn the oven down to 160°C/315°F/Gas 2½. Serve the quiche warm on its own, with celeriac rémoulade or salad.

Serves 6–8
Preparation time: 30 minutes, plus 25 minutes chilling and cooling
Cooking time: 50 minutes

FOR THE PASTRY
250g/9oz/2 cups plain flour, plus extra for dusting
125g/4½oz cold unsalted butter, diced
2 eggs
1 tbsp milk

FOR THE EGG & BACON FILLING
1 tbsp olive oil
1 skinless chicken breast, finely diced
30g/1oz unsalted butter, plus extra for greasing
1 onion, finely diced
2 thick smoked back bacon rashers, finely chopped
80g/2¾oz mature strong Cheddar, such as Snowdonia Cheese Black Bomber, grated
200ml/7fl oz/scant 1 cup double cream
55ml/1¾fl oz/scant ¼ cup milk
2 large eggs
sea salt and freshly ground black pepper

1 recipe quantity Celeriac Rémoulade (see page 217) or 1 recipe quantity Green Salad (see page 219), to serve

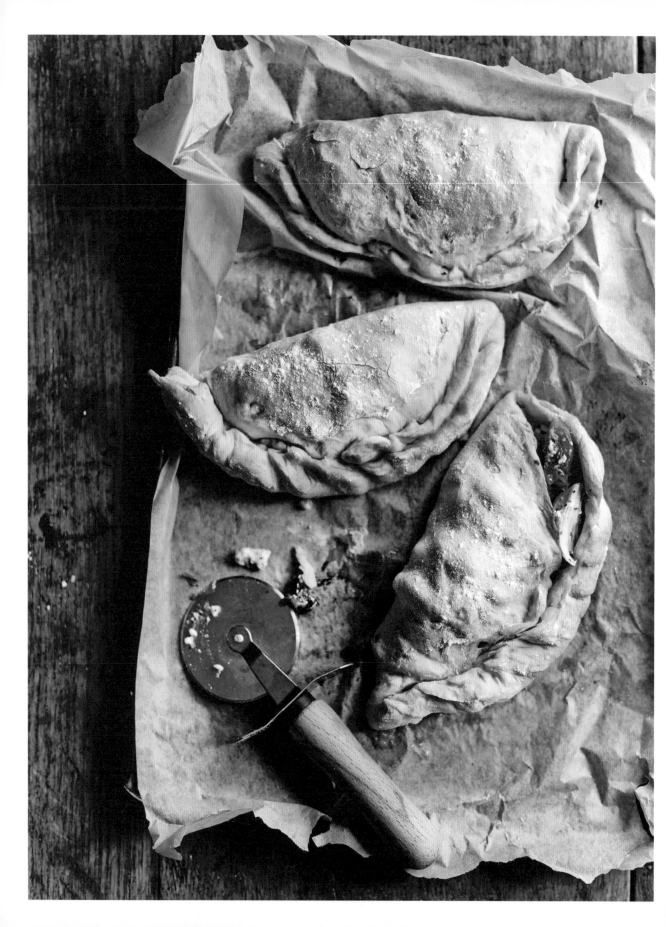

Chicken, cherry tomato, spinach & feta calzone

I'm sure you'll agree we all love pizza, and a calzone is pretty much a pizza dough pasty. Serve them like this with a salad to make a delicious main meal, or make eight calzone instead of four and serve them as a handy snack that will fill you up for a few hours. Try experimenting with all sorts of ingredients the next time you make them.

Preheat the oven to 200°C/400°F/Gas 6 and line two baking trays with baking paper. Put the chicken in a roasting tray and roast for 12–15 minutes until the juices run clear when the thickest part of the chicken is pierced with the tip of a sharp knife. Leave to stand for 5 minutes, then cut into small pieces.

Cut the pizza dough into quarters and roll out each piece on a lightly floured work surface into a circle about 1cm/½in thick. Put on the prepared baking trays.

Mix together the chicken and all the remaining ingredients, season with salt and pepper and gently toss together. Divide the filling among the pizza dough circles. Brush the edges with a little cold water, then fold half of the dough over the top and seal the edges together by twisting the pastry on itself.

Bake for about 15 minutes until golden. Serve warm or cold with a fresh salad.

Serves 4
Preparation time: 20 minutes, plus making the dough
Cooking time: 30 minutes

2 skinless chicken breasts, quartered
300g/10½oz Pizza Dough (see page 207)
a little flour, for dusting
200g/7oz feta cheese, diced
200g/7oz baby cherry tomatoes
1 tbsp chopped lovage or coriander leaves
50g/1¾oz baby spinach leaves
2 tbsp olive oil
sea salt and freshly ground black pepper
1 recipe quantity Microleaf & Carrot Salad (see page 219), to serve

Spinach & chicken ravioli with tomato sauce

Ravioli is a great combination of fresh pasta with, in this case, a meat filling, and I am serving it with a lovely rich sauce. Making fresh pasta is such a great technique to learn and it is so easy to do. If you like, you can make the ravioli in advance. Once sealed, you can freeze it before cooking, then simply cook it from frozen, making it really convenient for those looking for a nutritious meal in minutes.

Roll out the pasta on a lightly floured work surface to a thin rectangle about 0.5mm thick, or use a pasta machine.

Heat the oil in a frying pan over a medium-high heat. Add the chicken and fry for 4–5 minutes, stirring, until browned and cooked. Leave to one side to cool.

Rinse and drain the spinach, then put it in a saucepan with just the water clinging to the leaves. Put over a medium heat until softened, then drain and tip into a bowl to cool slightly. Add the chicken and the remaining stuffing ingredients to the bowl and mix until combined.

Spoon into a piping bag with a small, plain nozzle and pipe small round piles about the size of a cherry in lines over half the pasta, leaving about 4cm/1½in gap between each one. Dampen between the filling, then fold the other half of the pasta over to create a top sheet, carefully sealing between the ravioli and making sure you don't create any air pockets. Press out the ravioli, using a 4cm/1½in pastry cutter, pressing together the edges to seal.

Bring a large saucepan of water to the boil over a high heat, add the ravioli, in batches if necessary, and return to the boil. Simmer for about 6 minutes until just tender. Drain well.

Meanwhile, put the tomato sauce in a saucepan over a medium heat and bring just to the boil, stirring to make sure it is heated through. Add the ravioli and toss together to serve.

Serves 4
Preparation time: 30 minutes, plus
  making the dough and sauce
Cooking time: 20 minutes

1 recipe quantity Fresh Egg Pasta
  (see page 207)
a little flour, for dusting
1 recipe quantity Tomato Sauce
  (see page 199)

FOR THE STUFFING
2 tbsp olive oil
400g/14oz minced chicken
100g/3½oz spinach leaves
40g/1½oz unsalted butter, at room
  temperature
2 eggs
40g/1½oz strong cheese, grated
2 tbsp chopped chives
sea salt and freshly ground black pepper

Stuffed chicken thighs & egg noodles in cider cream

Succulent poached chicken and soft noodles bathed in a creamy cider sauce make a wonderful comfort dish – and it's so easy to make. If you can plan ahead, make the stuffed thighs in advance as you can keep them wrapped in the fridge for a day or two before you cook them.

Mix together the minced chicken and parsley in a bowl and season with salt and pepper. Lay a double layer of cling film on the work surface and put one of the chicken thighs in the centre. Open out the chicken thigh and put one-eighth of the mince down the centre, then roll the thigh to encase the stuffing and tie in three places. Roll the cling film around the chicken, pushing out any air as you do so, and tie each end securely in a knot. Wrap in the same way with kitchen foil. Repeat with the remaining thighs.

Bring a saucepan of water to the boil over a high heat. Put the chicken parcels into the water, turn the heat down to low and simmer for 10 minutes. Remove and leave to one side. Meanwhile, bring a large saucepan of water to the boil over a high heat, add the noodles and boil for 4 minutes until soft. Drain, then drizzle with the oil and keep warm.

To make the cider cream, melt the butter in a saucepan over a low heat. Add the shallots and cook for 2 minutes until soft, then stir in the flour and cook for 2 minutes. Gradually add the cider, whisking continuously to stop any lumps from forming, then gradually whisk in the stock and bring to a simmer. Add the thyme and cook for about 5 minutes, then add the cream and season with salt and pepper. Remove from the heat, cover and leave to one side.

Melt the butter in a large frying pan as you unwrap the thighs. Add them to the pan and fry for 1–2 minutes on each side until browned, in batches if necessary.

Add the noodles to the pan with a few spoonfuls of the sauce and warm through. Slice the chicken thickly and put on a bed of noodles with some extra cider cream spooned over. Serve with crusty bread.

Serves 4
Preparation time: 30 minutes, plus making the stock
Cooking time: 25 minutes

200g/7oz minced chicken
2 tbsp chopped parsley leaves
8 skinless boneless chicken thighs
300g/10½oz egg noodles
1 tbsp olive oil
1 tbsp unsalted butter
sea salt and freshly ground black pepper
crusty bread, to serve

FOR THE CIDER CREAM
50g/1¾oz unsalted butter
2 shallots, finely diced
30g/1oz/¼ cup plain flour
100ml/3½fl oz/scant ½ cup dry cider
400ml/14 fl oz/generous 1½ cups Chicken Stock (see page 197)
1 thyme sprig
3 tbsp double cream

Chicken & butternut squash gnocchi with sage butter

The first time I had gnocchi was when I went snowboarding in the Alps – it's the ideal dish for active people as it's a great source of carbohydrate to give you plenty of energy for the snowy slopes. I wanted to try a different spin on traditional gnocchi and as I really like the texture of butternut squash, I decided to add that to the chicken to make a dumpling. For this recipe, I have teamed the gnocchi with mushrooms and greens, but they would go equally well with one of my sauces, such as Fresh Basil Pesto (see page 201), or on their own as a starter for six.

Preheat the oven to 200°C/400°F/Gas 6. Put the butternut squash on a baking tray, drizzle with the oil, cover with kitchen foil and bake for 30 minutes until soft and tender.

Meanwhile, heat a non-stick frying pan over a medium heat. Add the chicken and cook for 3–4 minutes, stirring, until browned and cooked through. Transfer the squash to a blender and blend until smooth. Finely chop the chicken, then add it to the squash.

Tip the mixture into a bowl, add the flour and Parmesan, season with salt and pepper and bring the ingredients together until well blended. Turn onto a lightly floured work surface and roll into a sausage shape about 2cm/³⁄₄in in diameter. Cut into 2cm/³⁄₄in pieces using a sharp knife.

Bring a large pan of lightly salted water to the boil over a high heat. Add about 10 gnocchi and boil for a couple of minutes just until they float to the surface. Lift out with a slotted spoon and leave to one side to drain while you cook the remaining gnocchi.

Melt a little of the butter in a small pan over a medium heat. Add the mushrooms and fry for about 5 minutes until soft. Season with salt and pepper to taste. Meanwhile, heat the remaining butter in a frying pan over a medium-high heat. Add the gnocchi and sage and toss in the butter for a few minutes until golden.

Serve the gnocchi hot, straight from the pan, with the fried mushrooms and wilted greens.

Serves 4
Preparation time: 30 minutes
Cooking time: 45 minutes

400g/14oz butternut squash, peeled, halved and deseeded
1 tbsp olive oil
350g/12oz diced chicken
70g/2¹⁄₂oz/heaped ¹⁄₂ cup pasta flour, plus extra for dusting
20g/³⁄₄oz Parmesan cheese, grated
55g/2oz unsalted butter
2 tbsp chopped sage leaves
200g/7oz button mushrooms
sea salt and freshly ground black pepper
1 recipe quantity Wilted Greens (see page 217), to serve

Chicken, chorizo & butterbean casserole

This is really quick to put together, then you can just leave it in the oven to cook slowly until all the flavours have married perfectly. When I first made the dish on ITV's *This Morning* show, I planned to use belly pork, but we had to make a last-minute substitution because another chef had made a belly pork dish the day before, so we replaced the pork with chicken thighs. It was one of those moments when you change an element of a recipe because you've run out of that ingredient and you end up getting something even better than the original.

Preheat the oven to 160°C/315°F/Gas 2½. Heat half the oil in a flameproof casserole dish over a medium heat. Add the chicken and cook for a few minutes, stirring, until lightly coloured on all sides. Remove the chicken from the dish and leave to one side. Add the remaining oil to the pan with the onion, garlic and bacon and fry for 3–4 minutes. Stir in the smoked paprika and chorizo and cook for a further few minutes, stirring.

Add the red wine, tomatoes and tomato purée, return the chicken to the dish, then pour in enough water to just cover the ingredients. Cover with a lid or kitchen foil and bake for 1½ hours.

Stir in the butter beans, then cover and return the casserole to the oven for a further 20 minutes until the butter beans have soaked up the juices and heated through.

Remove from the oven and stir in the chopped spinach and half the coriander. Season with salt and pepper to taste, then gently stir together. Sprinkle with the remaining coriander and serve with steamed rice or chunks of fresh bread and butter.

Serves 4
Preparation time: 15 minutes
Cooking time: 2 hours

2 tbsp olive oil
500g/1lb 2oz skinless boneless chicken
  thighs, cut into chunks
1 onion, finely chopped
2 garlic cloves, crushed
90g/3¼oz smoked bacon or pancetta,
  diced
1 tsp smoked paprika
100g/3½oz chorizo, roughly diced
100ml/3½fl oz/scant ½ cup red wine
400g/14oz/scant 1²/₃ cups tinned chopped
  tomatoes
1 tbsp tomato purée
250g/9oz/heaped 1 cup drained tinned
  butter beans
100g/3½oz roughly chopped spinach
  leaves
2 tbsp roughly chopped coriander leaves
sea salt and freshly ground black pepper
steamed rice or chunks of bread and
  butter, to serve

Classic coq au vin

This classic chicken recipe has a great combination of flavours that makes for a lovely, rich, hearty stew – great to serve at any time of the year, but especially good on a cold winter's day. This is a particular favourite as I remember my mum making it when we were growing up.

Preheat the oven to 180°C/350°F/Gas 4. Season the chicken with salt and pepper, then dust in the flour. Heat the oil in an ovenproof frying pan or flameproof casserole dish over a high heat. Add the chicken and fry for about 10 minutes until lightly browned on all sides. Remove from the pan and leave to one side.

Turn the heat down to medium and add the butter. Add the onion and garlic and fry for 2 minutes. Add the bacon, mushrooms and shallots and fry for 3–4 minutes, then remove from the pan and add to the chicken.

Turn the heat up again, add the wine and deglaze the pan by stirring to remove any caramelized bits stuck to the bottom of the pan. Boil for 2 minutes until the wine has reduced by half, then add the stock and bring to the boil.

Return the chicken and bacon mixture to the pan, cover with a lid and bake for 35–40 minutes until the juices from the chicken run clear when the thickest part of the thigh is pierced with the tip of a sharp knife. Serve on its own or with boiled new potatoes.

Serves 4
Preparation time: 20 minutes,
  plus making the stock
Cooking time: 1 hour

4 chicken drumsticks, skin on
4 chicken thighs, skin on
40g/1½oz/⅓ cup plain flour
2 tbsp olive oil
2 tbsp unsalted butter
1 onion, finely diced
1 garlic clove, diced
2 thick smoked back bacon rashers,
  rind removed, finely diced
50g/1¾oz chestnut mushrooms,
  quartered
14 small round shallots or button onions
150ml/5fl oz/scant ⅔ cup red wine
500ml/17fl oz/2 cups Chicken Stock
  (see page 197)
sea salt and freshly ground black pepper
boiled new potatoes with butter and
  parsley, to serve

Chicken stroganoff with saffron-braised rice

Stroganoff was one of the first dishes I put on the menu when I first started cooking so it's a real nostalgia trip for me. To soak up all that lovely creamy sauce, my first choice is always to serve it with saffron rice, although you might prefer some freshly boiled plain rice.

Preheat the oven to 200°C/400°F/Gas 6. Melt the butter in a saucepan over a medium heat, add the onion and garlic and cook for 1 minute, stirring. Add the chicken strips and cook for 2–3 minutes on each side, then remove everything from the pan.

Return the pan to a high heat, add the brandy and deglaze the pan by stirring to remove any caramelized bits stuck to the bottom. Add the stock, bring to the boil and boil for 2 minutes until reduced to one-third. Stir in the cream, then the smoked paprika and cayenne.

Return the chicken and onion mixture to the pan and simmer for 5 minutes, stirring occasionally. Season with salt and pepper to taste, then add the parsley.

Meanwhile, melt the butter for the rice in an ovenproof saucepan over a medium heat. Add the shallots and cook for 2–3 minutes. Add the rice and cook for 1 minute, then add the stock and saffron, season with a little salt and pepper and bring to the boil. Cover with a lid and bake for 15 minutes until the rice is tender and all the liquid has been absorbed.

Stir the rice and season with salt and pepper to taste. Serve with the creamy stroganoff.

Serves 4
Preparation time: 20 minutes, plus making the stock
Cooking time: 20 minutes

30g/1oz unsalted butter
1 onion, finely diced
1 garlic clove, finely diced
4 skinless chicken breasts, cut into strips
3 tbsp brandy
100ml/3½fl oz/scant ½ cup Chicken Stock (see page 197)
100ml/3½fl oz/scant ½ cup double cream
1 tsp smoked paprika
¼ tsp cayenne pepper
1 tbsp chopped parsley leaves
sea salt and freshly ground black pepper

FOR THE SAFFRON-BRAISED RICE
50g/1¾oz unsalted butter
3 small shallots, finely diced
300g/10½oz/1½ cups long-grain rice
600ml/21fl oz/scant 2½ cups Chicken or Vegetable Stock (see page 197)
1 tbsp saffron strands

Thai green chicken & spinach curry with sag aloo

I'm a big fan of Thai spices like lemongrass and lime leaf – as you may have guessed if you have been trying out my recipes. They strike a lovely balance of freshness and flavour, with that spicy heat that rounds off the dish. Pairing it with an Indian dish may seem unlikely but it works.

Heat the oil in a large frying pan or wok over a medium-high heat. Add the curry paste and cook for 3–4 minutes, stirring. Add the chicken and cook for 3 minutes, then add the coconut milk and stock. Bring to the boil, then turn the heat down to low and simmer for 10–15 minutes until the chicken is cooked through. Add the green beans and cook for a further 3–4 minutes.

Meanwhile, to make the sag aloo, heat the oil in a frying pan over a medium heat. Add the onion and spices and cook for 3–4 minutes until softened and well blended. Add the potatoes and stir to coat in the spices, then add the baby spinach and cook for 1–2 minutes until softened.

Stir the spinach into the curry and serve with the sag aloo and some sticky rice.

Serves 4
Preparation time: 20 minutes, plus making the curry paste and stock
Cooking time: 30 minutes

2 tbsp olive oil
1 recipe quantity Thai Curry Paste (see page 205)
600g/1lb 5oz skinless boneless chicken thighs, cut into about 2cm/¾in pieces
300ml/10½fl oz/scant 1¼ cups coconut milk
400ml/14fl oz/generous 1½ cups Chicken Stock (see page 197)
100g/3½oz trimmed green beans
50g/1¾oz spinach leaves
sticky rice, to serve

FOR THE SAG ALOO
2 tbsp olive oil
1 onion, finely sliced
2 tsp ground cumin
1 tsp ground coriander
1 tsp turmeric
2 tsp garam masala
400g/14oz cooked potatoes, cut into chunks
100g/3½oz baby spinach leaves, roughly chopped

Kofta chicken & cashew nut curry

This is a beautifully mild, creamy curry sauce but still has plenty of flavour, with the smooth, rich taste of the cashews and chicken absorbing the warm spices. I like to serve it with saffron rice but boiled basmati rice is good, too. And perhaps add a few popadoms and mango chutney.

Mix together all the kofta ingredients, season with salt and pepper, cover and chill in the fridge for 30 minutes.

Meanwhile, toast the cashew nuts in a dry saucepan over a medium heat for a few minutes, tossing frequently, until lightly browned. Tip out of the pan onto a plate. Put half the cashews into a spice grinder or small food processor with the garlic, ginger, chilli and onion and 2–3 tablespoons water and blitz to a smooth paste. Leave to one side.

Remove the kofta mixture from the fridge and roll into walnut-sized balls. Heat half the clarified butter in a large frying pan over a medium heat. Add the koftas and fry for 4–5 minutes until cooked through and nicely browned on all sides. Remove from the pan and keep them warm.

Wipe out the pan, then return it to a medium heat and melt the remaining clarified butter. Add the garlic and onion paste and cook for a few minutes, stirring, until fragrant. Add the cumin, ground coriander and curry powder and cook for 1–2 minutes, stirring. Stir in 200ml/7fl oz/scant 1 cup water and add the bay leaf and cinnamon stick and a large pinch of salt and pepper. Bring to the boil, then turn the heat down to low and simmer for 2–3 minutes until the sauce has thickened and reduced slightly. Stir in the cream and cardamom.

Spoon a mound of saffron rice on each serving plate and top with the koftas. Spoon over some of the sauce and put the rest in a jug to serve separately. Sprinkle with the coriander leaves and the remaining cashew nuts and serve with a spoonful of mango chutney.

Serves 4
Preparation time: 15 minutes, plus 30 minutes chilling, and making the butter
Cooking time: 20 minutes

FOR THE KOFTAS

400g/14oz minced chicken
2cm/¾in piece of root ginger, peeled and finely chopped
1 tsp turmeric
2 tsp garam masala
2 garlic cloves, finely chopped
2 tbsp chopped coriander leaves
2 tbsp chopped mint leaves
sea salt and freshly ground black pepper

FOR THE KOFTA CURRY SAUCE

2 tbsp whole cashew nuts
2 garlic cloves
1cm/½in piece of root ginger, peeled and finely chopped
½ green chilli, deseeded
1 small onion, quartered
2 tbsp Clarified Butter (see page 196)
1 tsp ground cumin
1 tsp ground coriander
½ tsp Madras curry powder
1 bay leaf
½ cinnamon stick
80ml/2½fl oz/⅓ cup double cream
½ tsp ground cardamom

1 recipe quantity Saffron Rice (see page 210)
1 tbsp coriander leaves
Mango Chutney (see page 206), to serve

Moroccan chicken & chickpea tagine

North African-style recipes often feature sweet and savoury combinations, as does this Moroccan-inspired dish. If you don't have a Moroccan tagine – the distinctive conical Middle Eastern cooking pot – use any flameproof casserole dish.

Heat the oil in a tagine or flameproof casserole dish. Add the chicken and fry until just coloured on all sides, then remove from the dish, using a slotted spoon.

Add the onions and garlic to the dish and fry for about 3 minutes until softened, then stir in the spices and fry for 1–2 minutes until well blended. Stir in the chickpeas, raisins, tomatoes and lime leaf and return the chicken to the dish.

Cover and simmer for about 1 hour until the meat is tender and the sauce is thick. (Alternatively, cook in a preheated oven at 180°C/350°F/Gas 4 for the same length of time.)

When the tagine is almost ready, put the couscous in a heatproof bowl. Bring the stock to the boil in a saucepan over a high heat, then pour it over the couscous and stir well. Cover with cling film and leave to stand for 10 minutes until soft. Drain off any excess liquid.

Serve the chicken straight from the casserole dish on a generous pile of couscous.

Serves 4
Preparation time: 15 minutes, plus overnight soaking, and making the stock
Cooking time: 1¼ hours

2 tbsp olive oil
2 skinless chicken breasts, cut into chunks
4 skinless boneless chicken thighs, cut into chunks
2 onions, finely sliced
2 garlic cloves, finely chopped
1 tbsp smoked paprika
1½ tsp ground cumin
1 tsp turmeric
1 tsp peeled and grated root ginger
200g/7oz/scant 1 cup dried chickpeas, soaked overnight, then drained
80g/2¾oz/scant ⅔ cup raisins
400g/14oz/scant 1⅔ cups tinned chopped tomatoes
1 kaffir lime leaf
250g/9oz/1⅓ cups couscous
300ml/10½fl oz/scant 1¼ cups Vegetable Stock (see page 197)

Chilli chocolate chicken

This dish is full of flavour but not over-spicy, although if do you like your food hot, then you could add some chopped chilli or increase the amount of chilli powder in your version. Never be afraid to experiment and personalize recipes so they are exactly how you like them. Chilli and chocolate is a very ancient combination and well worth a try.

Heat the oil and butter in a large saucepan over a medium heat. Add the onion, garlic and red pepper and cook for 3–4 minutes until softened. Add the chicken and cook with the vegetables, stirring to break up the mince, for about 6 minutes until the chicken is lightly coloured.

Mix in the smoked paprika, chilli powder, tomatoes, kidney beans, stock and sugar, then bring to the boil, turn the heat down to low, partially cover with a lid and simmer for 45–60 minutes until the juices run clear when the thickest part of the chicken is pierced with the tip of a sharp knife and the sauce is thick. Season with salt and pepper to taste.

Spoon the chilli into bowls, then drop a piece of chocolate into each bowl and leave it to melt over the top. Serve with freshly baked bread.

Serves 4
Preparation time: 20 minutes,
  plus making the stock
Cooking time: 1 hour 10 minutes

1 tbsp olive oil
1 tbsp unsalted butter
1 large onion, finely diced
2 garlic cloves, finely chopped
1 red pepper, deseeded and finely
  chopped
500g/1lb 2oz minced chicken
1 tsp smoked paprika
1 tsp chilli powder
400g/14oz/scant 1⅔ cups tinned chopped
  tomatoes
400g/14oz tinned red kidney beans,
  drained
150ml/5fl oz/scant ⅔ cup Chicken Stock
  (see page 197)
1 tbsp dark soft brown sugar
100g/3½oz dark chocolate, 70% cocoa
  solids, broken into 4 pieces
sea salt and freshly ground black pepper
crusty bread, to serve

Chicken in a pot

It is said that this dish was originally created by King Henry IV of England so it has a royal pedigree. With lots of fresh vegetables, a light broth and beautifully juicy chicken, this twenty-first-century version is equally regal.

Bring the stock to the boil in a large, flameproof casserole dish over a high heat. Add all the vegetables and herbs for the broth. Put the whole chicken in the stock pot, reduce the heat to low, cover with a lid and simmer for 50 minutes until the juices run clear when the thickest part of the chicken is pierced with the tip of a sharp knife.

Carefully lift out the chicken, then strain the broth, discard the broth vegetables and return the broth to the casserole dish over a medium heat. Put the chicken back in the dish, add the prepared vegetables and season with salt and pepper to taste. Bring back to the boil, then turn the heat down to low, cover with a lid and simmer for a further 20–30 minutes until the vegetables are tender.

Lift out the chicken and carve it into portions. Serve with some of the vegetables and potatoes. Spoon a little of the broth over the top and sprinkle with the parsley and tarragon.

Serves 4–6
Preparation time: 15 minutes, plus making the stock
Cooking time: 1½ hours

FOR THE CHICKEN & VEGETABLE BROTH
1l/35fl oz/4 cups Chicken Stock (see page 197)
1 garlic bulb, cut in half horizontally
2 carrots, peeled and halved
2 celery sticks, cut into chunks
1 onion, quartered
2 leeks, trimmed and halved
1 bay leaf
1 bunch of parsley
2 thyme sprigs
10 black peppercorns
1 lemon verbena sprig

FOR THE CHICKEN
1 large chicken, about 2.5kg/5lb 8oz
4 carrots, peeled and cut into batons
3 leeks, trimmed and cut into chunks
2 small fennel bulbs, trimmed and cut into quarters
400g/14oz small new potatoes
2 tbsp chopped parsley leaves
1 tbsp chopped tarragon leaves
sea salt and freshly ground black pepper

Homemade chicken & pancetta sausages with mustard mash

Don't be put off by thinking it's difficult to make your own sausages – all you need are some sausage casings, which you can buy from your butcher or online. Your first attempts might be a bit lumpy but if you follow this recipe they'll taste great.

Mix together the minced chicken, pancetta, thyme, nutmeg, sugar, salt and pepper in a bowl, cover with cling film and chill in the fridge for at least 2 hours.

If you have a sausage maker, fill the skins with the meat mixture until you've used all the mince. If you don't have a sausage maker, spoon the mixture into a piping bag with a large nozzle and pipe the mixture into the sausage skins, twisting at even points along the long sausage. Cut into 8 individual sausages.

Heat the oil in a large frying pan over a medium-high heat. Add the sausages and fry for about 15 minutes, turning frequently, until browned and cooked through.

Meanwhile, bring a large saucepan of lightly salted water to the boil over a high heat. Add the potatoes, return to the boil, then turn down the heat and simmer for about 10 minutes until tender. Drain, then leave to air dry for a couple of minutes. Put them back in the pan, add the butter and mash until smooth, then mash in the mustard and cream and season with salt and pepper to taste.

Serve the sausages with the buttery mustard mash and a drizzle of red wine sauce.

Serves 4
Preparation time: 30 minutes,
  plus at least 2 hours chilling
Cooking time: 15 minutes

800g/1lb 12oz coarsely minced chicken,
  preferably thigh and breast meat
10 slices of pancetta, finely chopped
1 tbsp finely chopped thyme leaves
1 tsp grated nutmeg
1½ tsp caster sugar
1 tbsp sea salt
1 tbsp freshly ground black pepper
3 tbsp olive oil
1 recipe quantity Red Wine Sauce (see
  page 198), to serve

FOR THE MUSTARD MASH
700g/1lb 9oz floury potatoes, peeled and
  cut into small pieces
3 tbsp unsalted butter
2 tbsp wholegrain mustard
4 tbsp double cream
sea salt and freshly ground black pepper

Confit chicken with herb pearl barley

To confit chicken is basically slow cooking it in duck or goose fat or oil, and is a preserving method used for fish, meat – especially duck – and also some vegetables. The cooked meat becomes so tender that it just falls off the bone and it can be kept, covered in the fat or oil, in an airtight container in the fridge for up to a couple of weeks.

Preheat the oven to 100°C/200°F/Gas ½. Heat the sunflower oil in a large, ovenproof saucepan over a medium heat and add the juniper berries, peppercorns, cardamom, mustard seeds and 2 of the star anise. Bring to 85°C/176°F, so just below a boil. Carefully add the chicken legs so they are just covered in the oil. Cover with a lid, transfer to the oven and cook for 2½ hours. Insert a knife into the flesh. If it slips through to the bone, the legs are done. If not, return them to the oven for a further 30 minutes.

Carefully remove the chicken legs from the oil, taking care they don't fall apart, and drain on kitchen paper for 5 minutes. Discard the paper, cover the legs with cling film and chill in the fridge for up to 2 days, or until needed.

Meanwhile, rinse the pearl barley under cold running water, then drain and put in a saucepan with 200ml/ 7fl oz/scant 1 cup of the stock, the bay leaves and remaining star anise and bring to the boil over a high heat. Turn the heat down to very low and simmer for 20–25 minutes until cooked, stirring every 5 minutes. Remove from the heat.

Preheat or turn the oven up to 200°C/400°F/Gas 6. Put the chicken legs in a roasting tin, drizzle with a little of the olive oil and season with salt and pepper. Roast for 10–15 minutes until the chicken is golden and the skin crisp.

Heat the oil and butter in a large frying pan over a medium heat. Add the shallots and garlic, then the diced vegetables and sauté for a few minutes. Stir in the herbs and the cooked pearl barley with the remaining stock. Season with salt and pepper and bring to the boil, then simmer for 5–8 minutes until the vegetables are tender. Top the pearl barley with the chicken legs and serve with wilted greens.

Serves 4
Preparation time: 25 minutes, plus
  chilling (optional), and making the stock
Cooking time: 3 hours

3l/105fl oz/12 cups sunflower oil
8 juniper berries
12 black peppercorns
2 black cardamom pods
4 tsp mustard seeds
4 star anise
4 chicken legs, skin on
100g/3½oz/scant ½ cup pearl barley
600ml/21fl oz/scant 2½ cups Chicken
  Stock (see page 197)
2 bay leaves
2 tbsp olive oil
2 tbsp unsalted butter
2 shallots, sliced
4 garlic cloves, crushed
½ celeriac, peeled and finely diced
2 parsnips, peeled and finely diced
2 carrots, peeled and finely diced
leaves from 2 thyme sprigs, chopped
leaves from 2 rosemary sprigs, chopped
4 tsp chopped chives
sea salt and freshly ground black pepper
1 recipe quantity Wilted Greens
  (see page 217), to serve

Yakitori chicken with apricot bulgar wheat

Here I have combined flavours from two continents – the Japanese flavours of mirin, sake and soy with the Middle Eastern sweet fruits and grains. I love the fact that contemporary cooking has broken down so many barriers to experimenting with new ideas.

Put the bulgar wheat in a large heatproof bowl, then pour over the hot stock and leave to stand for 25–30 minutes. Soak some wooden skewers in cold water.

Meanwhile, put the marinade ingredients in a saucepan over a medium heat and warm gently until the sugar has dissolved, stirring occasionally. Pour into a bowl or jug, leave to cool slightly, then chill in the fridge for 15 minutes.

Put the chicken pieces into a bag or bowl and pour over the cooled yakitori marinade. Cover and leave to marinate in the fridge for about 30 minutes.

Preheat a griddle pan or barbecue until hot. Thread about 4 pieces of chicken on each skewer.

Drain any excess liquid from the wheat, then stir in the lemon zest and juice. Mix in the honey and chives, then the red onion and apricots. Season with salt and pepper to taste, then leave to one side.

Cook the skewers for 1–2 minutes on each side until cooked through and tender. Leave to rest for 1 minute, then serve with the apricot bulgar wheat.

Serves 4
Preparation time: 15 minutes,
  plus 1 hour soaking and marinating,
  and making the stock
Cooking time: 10 minutes

8 skinless boneless chicken thighs,
  cut into 2cm/³⁄₄in cubes

FOR THE APRICOT BULGAR WHEAT
125g/4¹⁄₂oz/²⁄₃ cup bulgar wheat
600ml/21fl oz/scant 2¹⁄₂ cups Chicken
  Stock (see page 197), boiling
grated zest and juice of ¹⁄₂ lemon
1 tbsp clear honey
2 tbsp chopped chives
1 red onion, finely sliced
200g/7oz/scant 1²⁄₃ cups ready-to-eat
  dried apricots, finely chopped
sea salt and freshly ground black pepper

FOR THE YAKITORI MARINADE
250ml/9fl oz/1 cup soy sauce
125ml/4fl oz/¹⁄₂ cup Chicken Stock
  (see page 197)
125ml/4fl oz/¹⁄₂ cup sake
125ml/4fl oz/¹⁄₂ cup mirin
50g/1³⁄₄oz/heaped ¹⁄₄ cup dark soft
  brown sugar

Teriyaki-glazed chicken breasts with sesame greens

Teriyaki is a traditional cooking method used in Japanese cuisine, consisting of cooking a piece of meat or fish using a sweet marinade, usually containing soy, mirin or sake, sugar and sometimes honey. When cooking, you should try to baste the meat at least once to give you a rich, sweet glaze. I've added a little garlic, ginger and Worcestershire sauce to give it extra flavour.

Whisk together all the marinade ingredients in a non-metallic bowl. Add the chicken breasts and turn to coat in the marinade, then cover with cling film and leave to marinate in the fridge for at least 1 hour.

Preheat the oven to 180°C/350°F/Gas 4. Heat the olive oil in a frying pan over a medium heat. Lift the chicken out of the marinade, add to the pan and fry for a few minutes on each side until browned.

Transfer to a roasting tin, brush with some of the remaining marinade, then roast for 12–15 minutes until the juices run clear when the thickest part of the chicken is pierced with the tip of a sharp knife. Cover with kitchen foil and leave to rest in a warm place while you cook the sesame greens.

To cook the sesame greens, heat the sesame oil in a frying pan or wok over a medium heat. Add the leeks, then the sugar snap peas and finally the courgettes and fry for 3–4 minutes, tossing together gently. Add the soy sauce and sesame seeds, season with salt and pepper and cook for a further 1 minute.

Serve the chicken and greens hot with some creamy mashed potatoes.

Serves 4
Preparation time: 15 minutes,
  plus at least 1 hour marinating
Cooking time: 25 minutes

4 skinless chicken breasts
1 tbsp olive oil
1 recipe quantity Creamy Mashed Potatoes
  (see page 212), to serve

FOR THE SESAME GREENS
2 tbsp sesame oil
2 leeks, trimmed and finely sliced
125g/4½oz sugar snap peas
2 courgettes, diced
2 tbsp light soy sauce
4 tbsp sesame seeds
sea salt and freshly ground black pepper

FOR THE TERIYAKI MARINADE
500ml/17fl oz/2 cups soy sauce
100ml/3½fl oz/scant ½ cup mirin or sake
4 tbsp dark soft brown sugar
2 garlic cloves, grated
1 tsp peeled and grated root ginger
1 tsp Worcestershire sauce

Crispy-skinned chicken with sweet potato purée, kale & crispy leeks

Great at anytime of the year, but I think real comfort food like this is ideal for those cold winter evenings. With the delicious crispy skin on succulent chicken, seasonal buttered kale and lovely crispy leeks on top, it'll banish those winter chills.

To make the sweet potato purée, bring a large saucepan of lightly salted water to the boil over a high heat. Add the sweet potatoes and boil for 10–15 minutes until tender. Drain, then transfer to a blender and blitz to a purée. Gradually blend in three-quarters of the butter, then the cream and season with salt and pepper to taste. Spoon into a saucepan, cover and leave to one side.

Preheat the oven to 180°C/350°F/Gas 4. Season the chicken with salt and pepper on both sides. Heat the oil in a large ovenproof frying pan, add the chicken, skin-side down, and fry for 2–3 minutes until golden. Turn the chicken over and cook for a further 2–3 minutes. Turn back onto the skin side and put the pan in the oven for 10–15 minutes until the juices run clear when the thickest part of the chicken is pierced with the tip of a sharp knife.

Meanwhile, make the crispy leeks. Put 3cm/1¼in of oil in a saucepan over a medium heat and bring to 180°C/350°F, when a cube of bread browns in 60 seconds. Season the flour with salt and pepper, then dust the leek in the seasoned flour. Lower about one-quarter of the leek into the hot oil and fry for about 2 minutes until crisp, then drain on kitchen paper. Keep it warm while you fry the rest.

To cook the kale, melt the remaining butter in a frying pan over a high heat. Add the kale and 3 tablespoons water and stir to steam the kale until softened. Turn the heat down and season with salt and pepper.

Warm through the sweet potato purée over a low heat. Remove the chicken from the oven, leave to rest for a minute, then slice on the diagonal. Serve with the sweet potato purée and kale.

Serves 4
Preparation time: 30 minutes
Cooking time: 35 minutes

2 large sweet potatoes, peeled and cut into small chunks
50g/1¾oz unsalted butter, diced
3 tbsp double cream
4 chicken supremes, skin on
1 tbsp olive oil, plus extra for frying the leek
100g/3½oz/heaped ¾ cup self-raising flour
1 large leek, trimmed and finely sliced into strips
250g/9oz kale, stalks removed
sea salt and freshly ground black pepper

Portuguese chicken with roasted garlic & pine nut & spinach

We used to spend our holidays at my grandparents' timeshare in Portugal, and everywhere you went they served the classic Portuguese piri piri chicken. So here's a simple dish to remind you of sun-drenched holidays.

Put all the marinade ingredients into a blender and blitz to a purée. Put the chicken breasts into a non-metallic bowl, cover with the marinade and rub it into the meat. Cover with cling film and marinate in the fridge for 1 hour.

Preheat the oven to 180°C/350°F/Gas 4. Toast the pine nuts in a dry saucepan over a medium heat for a few minutes, shaking the pan continuously, until they start to brown. Tip out of the hot pan and leave to one side.

Heat the oil in an ovenproof frying pan over a medium heat. Add the chicken breasts and fry for 2 minutes on each side. Transfer the pan to the oven and roast for 10 minutes until the chicken is cooked through and the juices run clear when the thickest part of the chicken is pierced with the tip of a sharp knife. Leave to rest while you cook the spinach.

Heat the butter in a saucepan over a medium heat, add the spinach and keep turning until the spinach starts to wilt. Add the toasted pine nuts, squeeze the roasted garlic cloves out of their skins into the pan and stir the spinach for 1–2 minutes until warmed through and mixed together but still retaining the bright green colour. Season with salt and pepper and serve with the chicken. Serve with a few fresh baby spinach leaves.

Serves 4
Preparation time: 15 minutes, plus 1 hour marinating, and making the roasted garlic
Cooking time: 20 minutes

4 skinless chicken breasts
50g/1¾oz pine nuts
1 tbsp olive oil
2 tbsp unsalted butter
200g/7oz spinach leaves
1 recipe quantity Roasted Garlic (see page 204)
sea salt and freshly ground black pepper
a few baby spinach leaves, to serve

FOR THE PORTUGUESE MARINADE
1 red onion, quartered
3 garlic cloves
1 red chilli with seeds
1 tbsp smoked paprika
1 tsp chopped thyme leaves
grated zest and juice of ½ lemon
½ red pepper, deseeded
1 tbsp olive oil
1 tsp salt

Roast chicken with mushroom & leek lentils

One of the reasons I love cooking is the vast range of interesting ingredients available. I'm a big fan of grains and pulses but sometimes they can be rather bland, so this is a great recipe to really show your guests that eating healthy grains and pulses isn't boring as long as you add lots of flavour during cooking.

Preheat the oven to 200°C/400°F/Gas 6. Bring the stock to the boil in a large saucepan over a medium heat, then turn the heat down to low and leave to simmer.

Melt half the butter in a large frying pan over a medium heat. Add the onion and garlic and cook for 3 minutes until softened. Stir in the lentils and the wine until absorbed.

Start to add 600ml/21fl oz/scant 2½ cups of the hot stock, a ladleful at a time, and cook, stirring continuously until the liquid has been absorbed before adding more. Repeat this process until all this stock has been absorbed. This should take about 20 minutes. Continue to cook the lentils for a further 10 minutes until they are just dry and gently caramelizing, stirring as they will start to stick to the base of the pan. Transfer to a bowl and leave to one side.

Season the chicken with salt and pepper on both sides. Heat the oil in a large ovenproof saucepan or wok over a medium heat. Add the chicken breasts, skin-side down first, and cook for 2–3 minutes on each side until just browned. Transfer the pan to the oven and roast for 20 minutes until the juices run clear when the thickest part of the chicken is pierced with a sharp knife.

Meanwhile, return the pan to a medium heat, add the remaining butter, the mushrooms and leeks and cook for 4 minutes until softened. Add the lentils and stir together well. Add half the remaining stock and stir until it is all absorbed, then add the remaining stock, the soy sauce, Worcestershire sauce, chives and thyme and cook for about 10 minutes until the lentils have a loose consistency like a risotto so it just holds its shape. Sit the chicken on top of the lentils, sprinkle with some parsnip crisps or crispy shallots and serve with wilted greens.

Serves 4
Preparation time: 20 minutes, plus making the stock
Cooking time: 45 minutes

800ml/28fl oz/scant 3¼ cups Chicken Stock (see page 197)
2 tbsp unsalted butter
½ onion, finely diced
1 garlic clove, finely diced
200g/7oz/1 cup Puy lentils, rinsed and drained
3 tbsp white wine
4 chicken breasts, skin on
2 tbsp olive oil
100g/3½oz mixed field mushrooms or wild mushrooms, finely sliced
100g/3½oz leeks, trimmed and finely sliced
2 tbsp light soy sauce
2 tsp Worcestershire sauce
2 tbsp chopped chives
1 tsp chopped thyme leaves
sea salt and freshly ground black pepper
1 recipe quantity Parsnip Crisps (see page 215) or Crispy Fried Shallots (see page 205), to serve
1 recipe quantity Wilted Greens (see page 217), to serve

Lemon verbena & thyme-roasted chicken

Brining a chicken is a great way to keep the meat moist when you are roasting, and it also flavours the meat. For my recipe, I'm using lemon verbena, but you can use lemon thyme instead. Either way, while it is cooking, the herbs make a pretty impressive aroma that everyone will appreciate. The number of servings obviously depends on the size of bird, but you can use the same principles and adjust the quantities if you have a smaller or a larger bird.

You will need a saucepan large enough to hold the chicken and brine and fit in the fridge. Put 6l/1.3 gallons/25 cups water in the pan, add all the brine ingredients and stir to dissolve the salt. Add the chicken, making sure that it is covered in the brine. Cover and leave in the fridge overnight, or for about 12 hours.

Preheat the oven to 160°C/315°F/Gas 2½. Remove the chicken from the brine and shake off any excess liquid. Stand it on a clean tea towel for a few minutes to drain, then pat the chicken dry. Pour the oil over the chicken and rub it into the skin, then season with salt and pepper.

Strain all the vegetables and herbs out of the brine and put the vegetables in a roasting tin and the herbs inside the chicken, then put the chicken on top. (I don't have the chicken trussed when roasting, so it cooks evenly throughout.) Roast for 1½ hours, then turn the heat up to 200°C/400°F/Gas 6 and roast for a further 15–20 minutes to get the skin crisp. The inside of the chicken closest to the bone should reach 70–77°C/158–170°F on a meat probe. If you don't have a probe, the juices should run clear when the thickest part of the thigh is pierced with the tip of a sharp knife. If there is any red or pink, cook for a little longer. Lift the chicken out of the tin, cover and leave in a warm place for 5–10 minutes while you make the gravy.

Put the roasting tray with the vegetables and juices over a medium heat. Add the red wine sauce and cook for 3–4 minutes, deglazing the pan by stirring to remove any caramelized bits stuck to the bottom. Strain through a fine sieve, then serve with the roast chicken, roast potatoes and wilted greens.

Serves 8
Preparation time: 20 minutes, plus 12 hours brining, and making the sauce
Cooking time: 2 hours

1 recipe quantity Brine (see page 17)
1 large chicken, about 2.5kg/5lb 8oz
2 tbsp rapeseed oil
1 recipe quantity Red Wine Sauce (see page 198)
sea salt and freshly ground black pepper
1 recipe quantity Roast Potatoes (see page 212), to serve
1 recipe quantity Wilted Greens (see page 217), to serve

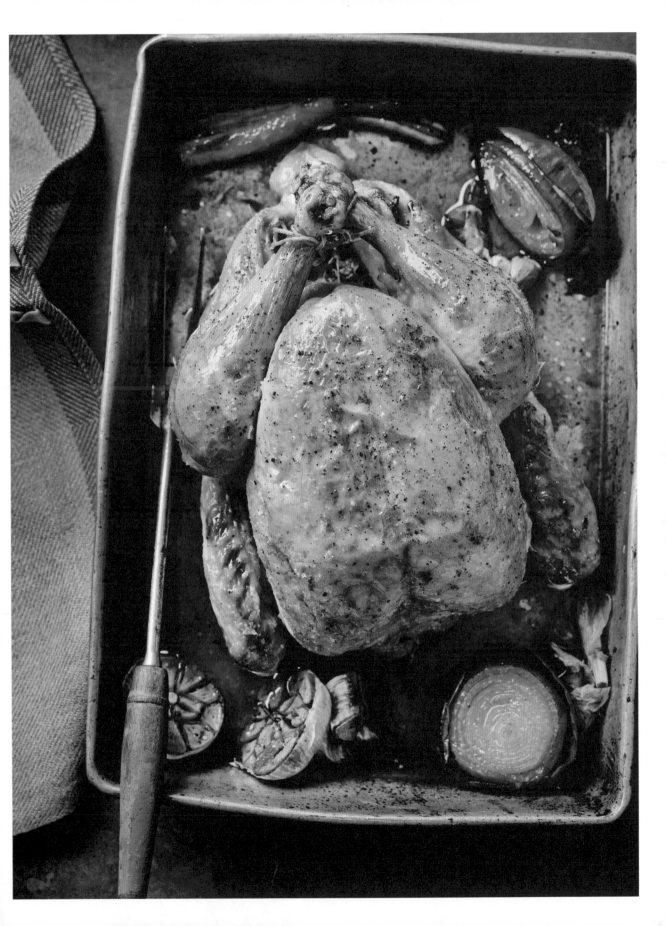

3

dinners &
celebrations

Chicken & watercress soup with vegetable crisps

Making a soup was one of the first things I did when I started cooking, building up the flavours from the base with onions or shallots and garlic sautéed in butter. If you want to become a good cook, start by making lots of soups and playing around with flavours and textures. This soup brings the peppery notes of watercress to the succulent chicken, with potato to thicken the soup and add both texture and flavour.

Melt the butter in a large saucepan over a low heat. Turn the heat up to medium, add the chicken, onion, garlic and leek and fry for 2–3 minutes until soft.

Add the potato, stock and half the watercress, bring to the boil over a medium heat, then turn the heat down to low and simmer for about 20 minutes until the potatoes are tender and the juices run clear when the thickest part of the chicken is pierced with the tip of a sharp knife.

Remove the chicken from the soup, shred into strips and leave to one side. Blend the soup until smooth, using a blender or food processor, then add the remaining watercress and the spinach and blitz again.

Return the soup and chicken to the rinsed-out pan. Bring to a simmer, then cook for 2–3 minutes until heated through. Drizzle with the cream, sprinkle with the thyme leaves and top with the sweet potato crisps. Serve with chunks of warm toast.

Serves 4
Preparation time: 15 minutes, plus making the stock and vegetable crisps
Cooking time: 30 minutes

50g/1¾oz unsalted butter
2 skinless chicken breasts, quartered
1 onion, finely sliced
1 garlic clove, finely diced
½ leek, trimmed and finely sliced
1 large floury potato, such as Maris Piper, peeled and diced
1l/35fl oz/4 cups Vegetable Stock (see page 197)
100g/3½oz watercress
100g/3½oz spinach leaves
2 tbsp double cream
1 tsp chopped thyme leaves
1 recipe quantity Sweet Potato Crisps (see page 215)
toast or crusty bread, to serve

Chicken, wild mushroom & miso soup

This recipe uses dashi stock, which can be used not only as a soup stock but also as a dipping sauce or a sauce for rice and noodles. It is made with kombu – a dried seaweed – and dried tuna flakes. You should find the ingredients in the major supermarkets or in oriental stores.

Soak the kombu in cold water for 30 minutes, then drain. Put in a saucepan, cover with 500ml/17fl oz/2 cups cold water and bring to the boil over a high heat. Just before the water boils, remove the kombu using a slotted spoon. Add the bonito flakes and return to the boil. As soon as the water returns to the boil, remove from the heat and leave to stand for about 10 minutes until the bonito flakes sink to the bottom, then for a further 5 minutes. Strain the stock into a clean pan and discard the bonito flakes and kombu. You should have 500ml/17fl oz/2 cups of the dashi stock.

Put the chicken, mushrooms, onion and carrots into the stock and bring to the boil over a high heat. Turn the heat down to low and simmer for 5–10 minutes until the vegetables are tender and the juices run clear which the thickest part of the chicken is pierced with the tip of a sharp knife. Add the spinach and tofu, if using, and simmer for 2 minutes until the spinach is softened.

Put the miso paste in a small bowl, add a ladleful of the soup from the pan and stir until blended. Gently stir this back into the soup. Remove from the heat and add the spring onions and the lime leaf. Serve with fresh bread or corn on the cob.

Serves 4
Preparation time: 20 minutes, plus 40 minutes soaking, and soaking the mushrooms
Cooking time: 20 minutes

FOR THE DASHI STOCK
10cm/4in piece of kombu
10g/1/2oz dried bonito flakes

FOR THE SOUP
2 skinless chicken breasts, each cut into 8 pieces
4 dried wild mushrooms, soaked overnight, then strained and finely chopped
1 onion, finely sliced
2 carrots, peeled and finely sliced into matchstick-sized pieces
50g/1¾oz baby spinach leaves, chopped
170g/6oz block of tofu, diced (optional)
3–4 tbsp miso paste
2 spring onions, diagonally sliced
1 kaffir lime leaf, finely chopped
fresh bread or corn on the cob, to serve

Deconstructed crispy pancetta & charred lettuce Caesar salad with anchovy straws

This is my modern version of a Caesar salad, with succulent chicken, crispy pancetta, a good free-range egg, crisp salad and rich dressing. With its contemporary twist, this looks a bit special to serve to your friends – and tastes fantastic. It is a dish that makes a great starter or a perfect light lunch, so you can adapt the quantities to suit your guests' appetites.

Preheat the oven to 180°C/350°F/Gas 4 and line a baking tray with baking paper. Put the pancetta on the prepared tray, cover with another piece of baking paper, then place a second tray on top. Bake for 10–12 minutes until golden brown. Transfer to a wire rack to cool and crisp.

Meanwhile, season the chicken with salt and pepper. Heat the oil in a frying pan over a medium-high heat. Add the chicken, skin-side down, and fry for 2–3 minutes on each side until golden. Transfer to a roasting tin and roast for 15 minutes until the juices run clear when the thickest part of the chicken is pierced with the tip of a sharp knife. Cover and leave to rest in a warm place until ready to serve.

While the chicken is cooking, bring a saucepan of water to the boil over a high heat. Gently lower the eggs into the water, then boil for 6½ minutes. Lift the eggs out of the water, using a slotted spoon, put in a bowl of ice-cold water to stop them from cooking further and leave to cool for about 5 minutes. Peel in the water, to stop them from breaking, then drain and cut in half.

Heat a griddle pan over a high heat. Add the lettuce, flat-side down, and cook for 1–2 minutes on each side. This gives the lettuce a charred effect and a slightly smoky flavour, but keeps it nice and crunchy in the centre.

Whisk together all the dressing ingredients in a non-metallic bowl until blended, then pour into small shot glasses. Slice the chicken and put on top of the lettuce halves, top with the eggs, sprinkle with the crispy pancetta and serve with the dressing and anchovy straws.

Serves 4
Preparation time: 20 minutes, plus making the mayonnaise
Cooking time: 25 minutes

8 slices of pancetta
2 chicken breasts, skin on, sliced in half
1 tsp olive oil
4 free-range eggs
2 Romaine lettuces, cut in half lengthways
sea salt and freshly ground black pepper
1 recipe quantity Anchovy Straws (see page 209), to serve

FOR THE CAESAR DRESSING
1 tsp anchovy paste
2 tbsp white wine vinegar
3 tbsp Mayonnaise (see page 202)
2 tbsp Dijon mustard
1 garlic clove, finely diced
½ tsp lemon juice
6 tbsp olive oil
2 tbsp grated Parmesan cheese

Chicken liver, orange, pea shoot & watercress salad

I used to hate chicken livers when I was growing up but over the years my palate has changed and now I love their soft texture. It is important to make sure you brown livers quickly but don't overcook them, otherwise they can go a bit dry. A touch of acidity helps to sharpen the flavour – I've used fresh orange segments to make this a great little salad for a starter or light lunch.

To make the croûtons, preheat the oven to 180°C/350°F/Gas 4. Cut the bread into long strips about 1–2cm/½–¾in thick, then cut across the strips to create cubes. Put on a baking tray, drizzle with the oil, sprinkle with the thyme and rosemary and season with the salt and pepper. Roast for 8–10 minutes until golden and crisp. Remove from the oven and leave to one side.

Slice off the top and bottom of the oranges, then peel from top to bottom, using a small, sharp knife, to remove all the skin and the white pith, leaving you with the orange still in shape but without its skin. Holding the orange in your left hand, you'll see the lines of the segments. Carefully slice lengthways on the inside of one of the lines to the centre then the same on the other side of the segment. The segment will just fall out. Repeat this with the whole of both oranges and leave to one side.

Put all the dressing ingredients in a bowl and whisk together until blended, then season with salt and pepper.

Heat the oil in a large frying pan over a high heat. Add the chicken livers and cook for 2–3 minutes without moving or shaking the pan. Turn the livers over and cook for a further 1 minute until the they are cooked but still slightly pink in the centre (cut one open to check), then remove the pan from the heat and add the butter. Baste the livers with the melted butter. Remove them from the pan and leave to rest on a warm plate.

Mix together the watercress and pea shoots in a bowl, add the croûtons, livers and orange segments, then drizzle over the dressing and toss together to serve.

Serves 4
Preparation time: 20 minutes
Cooking time: 15 minutes

2 large oranges
2 tbsp olive oil
400g/14oz chicken livers, trimmed
1 tbsp unsalted butter
30g/1oz watercress
30g/1oz pea shoots

FOR THE HERB CROÛTONS
2 thick slices of day-old crusty bread
1 tbsp olive oil
1 tsp chopped thyme leaves
1 tsp chopped rosemary leaves
1 tsp of sea salt
½ tsp crushed black peppercorns

FOR THE ORANGE DRESSING
2 tbsp balsamic vinegar
juice of 1 orange, about 60ml/2fl oz/¼ cup
60ml/2fl oz/¼ cup olive oil
½ tsp Dijon mustard
sea salt and freshly ground black pepper

Tea-smoked chicken & miso-dressed salad

I'm a big fan of smoked chicken, and by using green tea in your smoking ingredients, you retain the soft texture of the chicken and give it a more subtle smokiness. Add the lovely fresh chard, heritage tomato and cucumber and you get a super-light, fresh and summery salad with lots of colour and a smoky, crunchy texture from the bacon. If you can't buy chard, use a selection of rocket, beetroot leaves and sorrel. If you prefer, you can replace the bacon with 2 tablespoons of mixed pumpkin seeds, sunflower seeds or toasted peanuts.

Use a large saucepan with a steamer attachment. Line the saucepan with a double layer of kitchen foil, then empty the contents of the tea bags in the centre of the foil. Put the steamer on top and then the pan lid. Put the saucepan over a low to medium heat until you start to see the smoke rising into the steamer. Season the chicken breasts with salt and pepper, then put them in the steamer and cover with a lid. Leave to smoke for 30–40 minutes.

Meanwhile, if you are using the bacon, preheat the grill, Grill the bacon for 5 minutes until crisp, turning occasionally, then finely dice.

Put the tomatoes, cucumber and chard in a bowl and toss together lightly. Sprinkle with the diced bacon or the seeds or nuts.

Once the breasts are cooked, remove them from the steamer, cut into thin slices and add to the salad bowl. Sprinkle over the miso dressing to serve.

Serves 4
Preparation time: 20 minutes, plus making the dressing
Cooking time: 40 minutes

FOR THE TEA-SMOKED CHICKEN
8 green tea bags
4 skinless chicken breasts
sea salt and freshly ground black pepper

FOR THE TOMATO, CHARD & CUCUMBER SALAD
1 thick-cut smoked bacon rasher or 1 tbsp pumpkin or sunflower seeds or toasted peanuts
8 heritage tomatoes, sliced
1 cucumber, diced
10–12 mixed chard leaves, roughly chopped
1 recipe quantity Miso Dressing (see page 203)

Chicken, mushroom & baby leek terrine

I like the extra flavour of chestnut mushrooms but you can use ordinary mushrooms instead if you don't have them. The terrine takes very little time to put together but makes an attractive and flavoursome dish.

Bring a large saucepan of lightly salted water to the boil over a high heat. Add the leeks and boil for 2 minutes, then drain and put in a bowl of ice-cold water to stop them cooking further, then drain again and put in a roasting tin.

Melt the butter in a frying pan over a low heat. Add the mushrooms and fry for 2–3 minutes until just cooked but not losing their shape. Tip into the roasting tin and add the chicken, spinach, thyme and tarragon. Melt the duck fat, then pour it over the ingredients in the roasting tin and toss so they are coated in fat.

Line a 16 x 9cm/6¼ x 3½in terrine mould with cling film, leaving it overhanging the edges. Using a spoon so there is a little fat in each layer, start layering the ingredients into the terrine: chicken, then mushrooms, leek and spinach, seasoning each layer with salt and pepper, then repeat until the terrine is full. Wrap the cling film over the top, then press with a heavy weight, such as one or two full cans, and chill in the fridge overnight to set.

To serve, gently loosen the cling film around the edges of the mould and turn the terrine out onto a chopping board. Cut into slices using a knife dipped in boiling water, then serve with spiced apple chutney and homemade bread.

Serves 8
Preparation time: 30 minutes, plus overnight chilling, and making the confit
Cooking time: 10 minutes

150g/5½oz baby leeks, trimmed
30g/1oz unsalted butter
150g/5½oz chestnut mushrooms, halved
3 confit skinless chicken breasts (see page 122), sliced into long strips
50g/1¾oz baby spinach leaves
1 tsp chopped thyme leaves
1 tsp tarragon leaves
200g/7oz duck fat
sea salt and freshly ground black pepper
Spiced Apple Chutney (see page 206), to serve
homemade bread, to serve

Chicken, spinach, goats' cheese & slow-roasted tomato terrine

This makes a perfect summer starter, especially as you can prepare it in advance and have everything ready before your guests arrive. If you have some leftover chicken from a roast, you could use that instead of cooking the chicken.

Put the stock, half the butter and the bay leaf in a saucepan over a medium heat. Bring to the boil, then turn the heat down to low, add the chicken and simmer for 10–15 minutes until the juices run clear when the thickest part of the chicken is pierced with the tip of a sharp knife. Drain and leave to one side, reserving the stock.

Line a 16 x 9cm/16¼ x 3½in terrine mould with cling film, leaving it overhanging the edges. Melt the remaining butter in a saucepan over a medium heat. Add the spinach and cook for a few minutes, stirring, until just softened, then remove from the heat and leave to one side.

Warm the reserved stock in a saucepan over a medium heat. Soak the gelatine in a bowl of cold water until soft, then gently whisk into the stock.

Line the prepared mould with the Parma ham, leaving it overhanging the top enough to fold over and cover the top of the terrine. Start layering the ingredients into the terrine. Start with a layer of the chicken, then pour some of the stock over the top. Then make a layer of the tomatoes and moisten with stock. Next make a layer of the spinach and a little more stock, then finish with the crumbled goats' cheese. Season with salt and pepper and scatter in the herbs. Wrap the ham over the top. Wrap the cling film over the top, put a heavy weight on top, such as two full cans, and chill in the fridge overnight to set.

To serve, gently loosen the cling film around the edges of the tin and turn the terrine out onto a chopping board. Cut into slices using a knife dipped in boiling water, then serve with freshly baked bread.

Serves 8
Preparation time: 40 minutes, plus overnight chilling, and making the stock and slow-roasted tomatoes
Cooking time: 25 minutes

300ml/10½fl oz/scant 1¼ cups Chicken Stock (see page 197)
2 tbsp unsalted butter
1 bay leaf
3 skinless chicken breasts, each cut lengthways into 4
400g/14oz spinach leaves
4 sheets of gelatine
12 strips of Parma ham
300g/10½oz Slow-Roasted Tomatoes (see page 218) or sun-ripened tomatoes
100g/3½oz goats' cheese, crumbled
2 tsp chopped thyme leaves
2 tsp chopped chives
sea salt and freshly ground black pepper
fresh bread, to serve

Smoked chicken, mango & asparagus verrine

A verrine is a French dish in which the ingredients are layered in a small glass. I first discovered the verrine when I was doing some filming and was introduced to a lovely gentleman called Franc, who had written a book on them. I loved the visual aspect of it, with all the ingredients in one glass where the flavours marry together, and it works perfectly with smoked chicken and fresh asparagus in season to give you that lovely flavour of the countryside.

Bring a large saucepan of water to the boil over a high heat. Add the asparagus, return to the boil and simmer for 1 minute until just tender. Drain well, then put the asparagus into a bowl of ice-cold water to stop it from cooking further.

Meanwhile, bring another saucepan of water to the boil over a high heat. Gently lower the eggs into the water, then boil for 6½ minutes. Lift the eggs out of the water, using a slotted spoon, put in a bowl of ice-cold water to stop them from cooking further and leave to cool for about 5 minutes. Peel in the water, to stop them from breaking, then drain and dice.

Mix together the chicken, mayonnaise, tarragon and chives and season with salt and pepper. Cut off the tips of the asparagus spears, cut them in half crossways and leave to one side, then chop the rest of the asparagus stems into small pieces.

To assemble the verrine, have all your ingredients set out in front of you and have four wide 300ml/10½fl oz/ scant 1¼ cup tumblers handy. Start with a layer of the chicken mixture at the bottom of each tumbler, then a layer of mango, then chopped asparagus, then tomato and egg, then finish with the asparagus tips. Chill until you are ready to serve.

Serves: 4
Preparation time: 20 minutes, plus making the mayonnaise
Cooking time: 10 minutes

12 asparagus stems
2 eggs
2 smoked skinless chicken breasts (see page 144), cut into 1–2cm/½–¾in pieces
2 tbsp Mayonnaise (see page 202)
1 tsp chopped tarragon leaves
1 tbsp chopped chives
1 ripe mango, peeled, pitted and diced
3 vine tomatoes, deseeded and diced
sea salt and freshly ground black pepper

Confit chicken & charred pepper verrine

My second verrine uses the meltingly tender confit chicken – chicken legs cooked long and slow until they virtually fall apart. If you have some confit in the fridge, you can put this impressive starter together in no time.

Preheat the grill to high or use a gas flame to char the peppers over a naked flame for 3–4 minutes, turning until blistered and completely black. Put in a bowl, cover tightly with cling film and leave to one side for 5 minutes. Scrape off the skin with your fingers, then cut the flesh into very thin strips.

Meanwhile, put the shredded chicken in a bowl, mix with the mayonnaise, season with salt and pepper to taste and leave to one side. Holding the corn cob vertically on a chopping board, cut off the corn kernels, using a sharp knife, then discard the cobs.

To assemble the verrine, you will need four 300ml/ 10½fl oz/scant 1¼ cup glasses, preferably slightly wider at the bottom. Spoon some chicken into the bottom of the glasses, then a layer of peppers, then some rocket, then cherry tomatoes. Repeat the process, making sure you vary the pieces so the verrines look as colourful and appetizing as possible. Sprinkle with crispy shallots and serve.

Serves 4
Preparation time: 20 minutes, plus
 making the confit and mayonnaise
Cooking time: 5 minutes

1 red pepper
1 green pepper
4 confit chicken legs (see page 122),
 shredded
3 tbsp Mayonnaise (see page 202)
2 cooked corn cobs
100g/3½oz rocket leaves
12 cherry tomatoes, halved
sea salt and freshly ground black pepper
1 recipe quantity Crispy Fried Shallots
 (see page 205), to serve

Courgette, chicken & mozzarella tempura

Perfect for an impressive canapé or even just a simple snack, courgette flowers have a lovely, delicate flavour and texture. The innovative twist in this recipe is created by stuffing them with a finely chopped chicken mixture, and dipping them in a tempura batter before deep-frying. You end up with a very light, crispy batter surrounding the tender chicken.

Put the chicken thighs in a saucepan and just cover with water. Bring to the boil over a high heat, then turn the heat down to low and simmer for 30–40 minutes until the juices run clear when the thickest part of the chicken is pierced with the tip of a sharp knife. Drain and leave to cool, then chop finely.

Mix together the chicken, rocket, mozzarella, cream cheese and chives and season with salt and pepper. Divide into 4 equal balls and put one inside each courgette flower, pinching the tops to make them into little parcels.

Mix together the flour and cornflour with a pinch of salt, then gradually add enough of the soda water to create a light batter.

Heat the groundnut oil in a deep, heavy-based saucepan to 180°C/350°F, when a cube of day-old bread will brown in 40 seconds. Dip the courgette flowers into the batter, then deep-fry, in batches if necessary, for about 2 minutes until crisp and golden. Drain well on kitchen paper and season lightly with salt and pepper before serving.

Serves 4
Preparation time: 15 minutes,
  plus cooling
Cooking time: 45 minutes

3 skinless boneless chicken thighs
100g/3½oz rocket leaves, chopped
100g/3½oz buffalo mozzarella, chopped
60g/2¼oz cream cheese
2 tbsp chopped chives
4 large courgette flowers
groundnut oil, for deep-frying
sea salt and freshly ground black pepper

FOR THE TEMPURA BATTER
100g/3½oz/heaped ¾ cup self-raising
  flour
1 tbsp cornflour
150–185ml/5–6fl oz/scant ⅔–¾ cup cold
  soda water

Chicken liver & sweet wine jelly parfait

Chicken liver has a delicate flavour and soft texture that makes a subtle introduction to any meal, and here it is made into a particularly creamy parfait. The contrast with the sweet jelly and the slight sharpness of the orange zest set the flavours off perfectly.

Lightly oil a 18cm/7in round cake tin and line it with cling film. Melt half the clarified butter in a frying pan over a medium heat. Add the shallots and fry for 3 minutes until just browned, then tip into a blender.

Reheat the pan, add the remaining clarified butter and the livers and cook for 2 minutes on each side until brown on the outside but still just pink in the centre. Scrape the livers and butter into the blender with the shallots.

Put the pan back on the heat and carefully add the brandy. Don't stand too close as it is could set alight. Deglaze the pan by stirring to remove any caramelized bits stuck to the bottom, then scrape everything into the blender with the other ingredients. Add the cream and season well with salt and pepper. Blitz until gently puréed. With the blender running, gradually add the butter, a piece at a time, until it is all combined. Spoon the mixture into the prepared tin, cover with cling film and chill in the fridge for at least 4 hours until set. Put the grapes on a baking tray and freeze for at least 2 hours.

Once the parfait is just set, make the jelly. Put the gelatine sheets in a bowl of cold water and leave to soak for a few minutes until soft. Put the wine in a saucepan over a low heat to warm through – you don't want it to boil – then remove from the heat and add the orange zest. Slowly and gently whisk in the gelatine sheets one at a time. Transfer to a jug and leave to cool for 5–10 minutes. Gently pour the sweet wine jelly on top of the parfait, then cover and return it to the fridge for at least 2 hours to set.

To serve, gently loosen the cling film around the edges and turn the parfait out onto a chopping board. Cut into cake-style wedges using a knife dipped in boiling water, then serve with fresh bread or toast and the frozen grapes.

Serves 4–6
Preparation time: 30 minutes, plus at least 6 hours chilling, and making the butter
Cooking time: 20 minutes

a little oil, for greasing
50g/1¾oz Clarified Butter (see page 196)
30g/1oz shallots, finely sliced
350g/12oz chicken livers, trimmed
1 tbsp brandy
1 tbsp double cream
210g/7½oz unsalted butter, softened and diced
30 green or red seedless grapes, cut into bunches of 5
6 sheets of gelatine
150ml/5fl oz/scant ⅔ cup sweet Muscat wine
grated zest of 1 orange
sea salt and freshly ground black pepper
fresh bread or toast, to serve

Potted chicken & spiced butter with caramelized shallot jam

Potted meat might sound a bit old-fashioned but don't be fooled – this brings it alive with a contemporary twist of nutmeg and cayenne plus a lovely, sticky-sweet preserve. Not only are potted dishes a useful way to preserve meat, they are ideal if you want an appetizer that you can make in advance. I use confit chicken as it is very soft and delicate and works perfectly set in the spiced butter.

First, make the spiced butter, Melt the butter in a saucepan over a low heat. Remove from the heat and leave to settle, then gently pour off the clear butter into a jug, making sure you leave behind the white fats floating on the top or at the bottom. Whisk in the nutmeg, cayenne and mace, then leave to one side.

Put the shredded meat in a bowl, mix in the parsley and season with salt and pepper to taste. Divide the mixture into four ramekins dishes, filling them just over half full, then slowly pour over the spiced butter. Place on a tray and chill in the fridge for about 1 hour.

To make the shallot jam, heat the oil in a saucepan over a medium heat, add the shallots and fry for 3–4 minutes until softened. Add the vinegar, sugar and thyme and 100ml/3½fl oz/scant ½ cup water, bring to the boil, then turn the heat down to low and simmer for about 10 minutes, stirring occasionally, until reduced, thickened and slightly caramelized. Serve the potted chicken with a spoonful of shallot jam and fresh crusty rolls.

Serves 4
Preparation time: 15 minutes, plus 1 hour chilling, and making the confit
Cooking time: 20 minutes

FOR THE SPICED BUTTER
250g/9oz unsalted butter
½ tsp grated nutmeg
a small pinch of cayenne pepper
a small pinch of ground mace

FOR THE CHICKEN
1 confit chicken leg (see page 122), boned and shredded
1 tbsp chopped parsley leaves
sea salt and freshly ground black pepper
4 homemade or shop-bought crusty rolls, toasted, to serve

FOR THE CARAMELIZED SHALLOT JAM
1 tbsp olive oil
300g/10½oz banana shallots, finely sliced
2 tsp red wine vinegar
2 tbsp dark soft brown sugar
1 tsp chopped thyme leaves

Chicken & prawn dumplings with soy dipping sauce

I've always been a 'grazer' (it stems from tasting lots of dishes during service and generally not having time for proper sit-down meals), so this is just the dish for me – these little dumplings make healthy snack food that's perfect for sharing with friends. If you use a bamboo steamer, you can serve the dumplings straight from the steamer.

Mix together the chicken, prawns, salt and pepper in a bowl. Add all the remaining dumpling filling ingredients except the wrappers and mix together. Cover the bowl with cling film and chill in the fridge for 30 minutes to firm up.

Put a teaspoonful of filling on the first wonton wrapper, bring up the sides and press them around the filling mixture. Tap the dumpling on a flat surface to make the bottom flat, then repeat the process until you have used all the mixture.

Put a large saucepan of water on to simmer, with a steamer insert on top. Put the dumplings into the steamer and cook for 5–10 minutes until tender and cooked through.

Meanwhile, mix together all the dipping sauce ingredients in a non-metallic bowl.

Serve the dumplings straight from the steamer with the dipping sauce served separately.

Serves 4
Preparation time: 20 minutes, plus 30 minutes chilling
Cooking time: 10 minutes

FOR THE CHICKEN & PRAWN DUMPLINGS
250g/9oz minced chicken
250g/9oz raw peeled tiger prawns, finely chopped
1 tsp salt
1 tsp freshly ground black pepper
4 tbsp chopped coriander leaves
100g/3½oz water chestnuts, finely chopped
2 tbsp soy sauce
2 tbsp finely chopped spring onions
1 tbsp mirin
1 tsp caster sugar
2 tsp sesame oil
200g/7oz wonton wrappers

FOR THE SOY DIPPING SAUCE
4 tbsp light soy sauce
4 tbsp Chinese rice vinegar
4 tsp toasted sesame oil
2 tbsp finely chopped coriander leaves

Chicken meatballs with lime leaf, cardamom & coconut dipping sauce

The influence of Indonesian chicken satay was the starting point for this dish, married with the fact that I enjoy deep-fried meat with a simple sauce. You can also serve the sauce with simple chargrilled or barbecued chicken.

Heat the oil in a large saucepan over a medium heat. Add the chicken and fry for 1–2 minutes on each side until brown. Add the stock and bring to the boil, then turn the heat down to low and simmer for 2 hours until the meat is falling off the bone. Drain and leave to one side to dry.

To make the sauce, heat the sesame oil in a saucepan over a medium heat, add the garlic and chillies, then add all the spices and cook for 2–3 minutes, stirring continuously. Stir in the peanuts, then the coconut cream, ginger and sugar and cook, stirring regularly, for about 15 minutes until thick and well blended. (You can make it in advance and store in a screw-topped jar in the fridge until needed.)

To make the batter, mix together the flour and cornflour in a bowl, then gradually whisk in the sparkling water until you have a light batter, the consistency of lightly whipped cream. Season with salt and pepper and leave to one side.

Shred the chicken and mix with the spring onions and mustard, season with salt and pepper and shape into balls the size of a small plum. Heat the groundnut oil in a saucepan to 180°C/350°F, when a cube of bread browns in 50 seconds. One at a time, dip 4 meatballs into the batter and gently lower into the hot oil. Cook for about 2 minutes, turning occasionally to cook evenly, then remove from the pan, using a slotted spoon, and drain on kitchen paper. Keep them warm while you cook the remaining meatballs.

To give the presentation something a little bit special after deep-frying, skewer the meatballs through the centre with a bamboo cocktail stick, keeping the stick exposed on both sides. Put the coconut dipping sauce in a shot glass and sit your meatball on top of the glass.

Serves 4
Preparation time: 30 minutes, plus making the stock
Cooking time: 2½ hours

2 tbsp olive oil
6 skinless chicken thighs
500ml/17fl oz/2 cups Chicken Stock (see page 197)
2 tbsp chopped spring onions
1 tbsp Dijon mustard
500ml/17fl oz/2 cups groundnut oil, for deep-frying
sea salt and freshly ground black pepper

FOR THE COCONUT DIPPING SAUCE
2 tbsp sesame oil
5 garlic cloves, finely chopped
2 red chillies, deseeded and chopped
1 tsp finely chopped lemongrass stalk
2 kaffir lime leaves, finely chopped
1 black cardamom pod, crushed to a powder
1 tsp ground cumin
100g/3½oz/scant ⅔ cup unsalted shelled roasted peanuts
375ml/13fl oz/1½ cups coconut cream
1 tsp peeled and grated root ginger
2 tsp caster sugar

FOR THE BATTER
100g/3½oz/heaped ¾ cup self-raising flour
25g/1oz/¼ cup cornflour
150–185ml/5–6fl oz/scant ⅔–¾ cup cold sparkling water

Chicken, corn & prawn balls

Chicken, corn and prawns make a great combination, especially in these crunchy meatballs created by egg-washing and breadcrumbing the meat mixture – add a spicy chilli sauce and you have a great dish.

Put the chicken and prawns into a blender and pulse until minced, then turn into a bowl. Add all the other meatball ingredients and combine together. Cover with cling film and chill in the fridge for 30 minutes.

Divide and shape the mixture into 8 balls. Whisk together the eggs and milk in a shallow bowl to make an egg wash and put the breadcrumbs in a second bowl. Dip the meatballs in the egg wash, shake off any excess, then roll in the breadcrumbs.

Heat the groundnut oil in a deep, heavy-based saucepan to 180°C/350°F, when a cube of bread browns in 50 seconds. Gently lower the meatballs into the oil, a few at a time, and deep-fry for 2–3 minutes, turning occasionally so they cook evenly, then remove from the pan, using a slotted spoon, and drain on kitchen paper. Keep them warm while you cook the remaining meatballs.

Serve the meatballs with sweet chilli sauce and a red onion, chive and tomato salad.

Serves 4
Preparation time: 20 minutes,
  plus 30 minutes chilling
Cooking time: 15 minutes

FOR THE CHICKEN, CORN & PRAWN MEATBALLS

2 skinless chicken breasts
2 skinless boneless chicken thighs
150g/5^{1}/$_{2}$oz raw peeled tiger prawns
100g/3^{1}/$_{2}$oz/^{1}/$_{2}$ cup drained tinned
  sweetcorn kernels
4 spring onions, finely diced
2 red chillies
1 lemongrass stalk, finely chopped
1 tbsp peeled and finely diced root ginger
2 tbsp panko breadcrumbs
1 tbsp chopped coriander leaves
1 tbsp chopped chives
1 egg
1 tbsp olive oil

FOR THE COATING

2 eggs
2 tbsp milk
100g/3^{1}/$_{2}$oz/1 cup panko breadcrumbs

groundnut oil, for deep-frying
1 recipe quantity Sweet Chilli Sauce
  (see page 161), to serve
red onion, chive and tomato salad,
  to serve

Vietnamese chicken & pomegranate seed wraps with sweet chilli sauce

Asian-style finger food makes a sociable and deliciously relaxed starter to any meal. The chicken leg meat gives a great depth of flavour and I like the fact that it remains moist and doesn't dry out when cooking. Crisp bean sprouts, aromatic coriander and the unusual addition of crunchy pomegranate seeds complete this winning dish.

Preheat the oven to 180°C/350°F/Gas 4. Heat the oil in a frying pan over a medium-high heat. Season the chicken with salt and pepper, then add to the pan and fry for 1–2 minutes on each side until brown. Transfer to a roasting tin and roast for 12 minutes until the juices run clear when the thickest part of the chicken is pierced with the tip of a sharp knife. Remove from the oven and leave to cool slightly, then remove all the meat from the bones and chop finely, then put the meat in a bowl.

Mix together the bean sprouts, chilli, cucumber, carrot, spring onions and coriander in a bowl. Hold the pomegranate halves over the bowl and bash the outer skin with a wooden spoon until all the seeds fall into the bowl.

Add the sesame oil and soy sauce, then season with salt and pepper and mix together until combined.

Submerge the rice paper wrappers in warm water and leave to soak for 1 minute, then lay them out on a board. Take care as they are quite fragile. Put 1–2 spoonfuls of the pomegranate mixture and the chicken down the centre of a wrapper. Fold the wrapper over the filling, tuck in the ends, then roll the wrapper until it forms a spring roll shape. Continue until you have used all the wrappers and filling mixtures.

Mix together the ingredients for the chilli dipping sauce and serve with the wraps. Then just dig in and enjoy your delicious creation.

Serves 4–5
Preparation time: 30 minutes
Cooking time: 15 minutes

1 tbsp olive oil
4 chicken drumsticks
100g/3½oz bean sprouts
1 chilli, deseeded and cut into thin strips (optional)
½ cucumber, cut into matchstick-sized pieces
1 carrot, peeled and sliced into matchstick-sized pieces
4 spring onions, finely sliced into rings
4 tbsp finely chopped coriander leaves
1 pomegranate, halved
1 tsp sesame oil
1 tsp light soy sauce
8 rice paper wrappers
sea salt and freshly ground black pepper

FOR THE SWEET CHILLI SAUCE
4 tbsp light soy sauce
2 tsp rice vinegar
1 tsp caster sugar
½ tsp peeled and finely grated root ginger
½ tsp dried chilli flakes
1 tsp sesame seeds

Chicken in filo cones with orange salad

This is an impressive way of presenting a simple salad by filling crispy filo cones with chicken meat and serving them with a tangy orange salad. It makes a delightful starter or even a summer lunch, or you could make smaller cones and serve as stylish canapés.

Cut a 25cm/10in circle out of thin card, roll into a cone shape and secure with staples to make a mould. Wrap the mould in kitchen foil, then remove the card and repeat to make three more foil cones.

Slice off the top and bottom of the oranges, then peel from top to bottom, using a small, sharp knife, to remove all the skin and the white pith, leaving you with the orange still in shape but without its skin. Holding the orange in your left hand, you'll see the lines of the segments. Carefully slice lengthways on the inside of one of the lines to the centre, then the same on the other side of the segment. The segment will just fall out. Repeat this with the whole of both oranges, reserving the juice.

Preheat the oven to 180°C/350°F/Gas 4. Use 2 sheets of filo pastry to wrap a double layer of filo around each cone, brushing with melted clarified butter where the sheets overlap. Brush with melted clarified butter and sprinkle with black sesame seeds. Put on a baking tray and bake for about 4 minutes until golden and cooked. Remove from the oven and leave to cool before removing the foil cone.

Mix together the chicken, mayonnaise, chives and 1 tablespoon of the reserved orange juice in a bowl, and season to taste with salt and pepper.

Mix together the orange segments and salad leaves, season with salt and pepper and drizzle with a little salad dressing. Carefully fill the filo cones with the chicken mixture and serve with the orange salad.

Serves 4
Preparation time: 30 minutes, plus making the confit, butter, mayonnaise and dressing
Cooking time: 5 minutes

2 oranges
8 sheets of filo pastry
2 tbsp Clarified Butter (see page 196), melted
2 tbsp black sesame seeds
3 confit chicken legs (see page 122) or poached chicken breasts (see page 23), shredded
3 tbsp Mayonnaise (see page 202)
2 tbsp chopped chives
200g/7oz baby salad leaves
a drizzle of Bean House Salad Dressing (see page 203)
sea salt and freshly ground black pepper

Chicken, goats' cheese & red onion tarte tatin

Tarte tatin is a classic French recipe for an apple tart cooked upside-down, supposedly invented when a pie was dropped on the floor. This is my modern twist as it is a savoury version that combines mellow goats' cheese and sweet red onions.

Roll out the pastry on a lightly floured work surface until it is about 5cm/2in larger than a 23cm/9in ovenproof frying pan. Cover with a clean, damp tea towel and leave to one side.

Preheat the oven to 180°C/350°F/Gas 4. Melt the butter in the frying pan over a low heat, add the thyme, vinegar and sugar and cook for a few minutes until the sugar has dissolved. Add the onions, cut-side down, and cook for 3–5 minutes until soft. Add the chicken in between the onions and cook for 8–10 minutes until the chicken is cooked through. Sprinkle with the cheese.

Remove the pan from the heat. Carefully lift the pastry and put it over the top of the chicken mixture, tucking in the sides so nothing escapes. Whisk together the egg and milk to make an egg wash and brush over the pastry, then bake for 20 minutes until the pastry is golden brown.

Carefully put a plate, slightly larger than the frying pan, on top of the pan, then invert the tart onto the plate so the pastry is at the bottom. Serve with buttered potatoes and green vegetables.

Serves 4
Preparation time: 15 minutes, plus making the pastry (optional)
Cooking time: 35 minutes

220g/7¾oz Rough Puff Pastry (see page 208) or puff pastry, thawed if frozen
a little flour, for dusting
40g/1½oz unsalted butter
1 tbsp thyme leaves
2 tbsp balsamic vinegar
125g/4½oz/heaped ½ cup caster sugar
8 small red onions, halved
2 skinless chicken breasts, finely sliced
100g/3½oz goats' cheese
1 egg
1 tbsp milk
boiled and buttered new potatoes and steamed green vegetables, to serve

Chicken Wellington with honey-roasted root vegetables

I couldn't resist trying a chicken version of that classic, beef Wellington, as pastry and meat are just made to go together. It goes with almost any vegetables, but these honey-roasted root vegetables are my first choice. The fillets that are removed are the thin strips underneath the chicken breasts – use them for another dish.

Preheat the oven to 190°C/375°F/Gas 5. Rinse and drain the spinach, then put it in a saucepan with just the water clinging to the leaves. Put over a medium heat until softened, then drain.

Quarter the pastry, then roll each piece into a 20cm/8in diameter circle on a lightly floured work surface. Beat together the egg and milk to make an egg wash.

Lay 2 slices of pancetta on the work surface, put a chicken breast on top, then one-quarter of the spinach and wrap the pancetta tightly round the chicken. Put the wrapped chicken breast on the pastry, brush the edges with egg wash and roll the pastry around the chicken, sealing the edges of the pastry and making sure there are no gaps. Repeat to make the remaining chicken Wellingtons.

Put the chicken Wellingtons onto a baking tray, brush with the egg wash all over and bake for 25–30 minutes until cooked through.

Leave the Wellingtons to rest for 2 minutes, then serve with the roasted vegetables and a little gravy or sauce.

Serves 4
Preparation time: 30 minutes,
  plus making the pastry (optional)
Cooking time: 30 minutes

200g/7oz spinach leaves
200g/7oz Rough Puff Pastry (see page 208)
  or puff pastry, thawed if frozen
a little flour, for dusting
1 egg
1 tsp milk
8 slices of pancetta
4 skinless chicken breasts, fillets removed
1 recipe quantity Honey-Roasted Root
  Vegetables (see page 216)
1 recipe quantity Traditional Chicken
  Gravy or Red Wine Sauce (see page 198),
  to serve

Chicken, mushroom & red parsley suet pudding

Japanese red parsley, or mitsuba, has a flavour something like celery and is not actually red. If you cannot find it, just use flat-leaf parsley instead. This is a hearty dish that may stretch to six guests if you serve it with a generous serving of seasonal vegetables.

Season the flour with salt and pepper, then coat the chicken in the flour. Melt the butter in a heavy-based saucepan over a low heat. Add the chicken and fry for 2–3 minutes on each side until lightly browned. Remove from the pan and leave to one side.

Heat the oil in the same pan over a high heat, add the onion and fry for 3–4 minutes, then add the garlic and mushrooms and fry for 1 minute, stirring. Return the chicken to the pan and add the herbs and stock. Bring to the boil, then reduce the heat to low, cover the pan and simmer for 1½ hours. Leave to cool.

To make the pastry, combine all the dry ingredients in a bowl, then gradually add 170ml/5½fl oz/⅔ cup water and bring together to a dough. Knead gently on a lightly floured work surface for 1 minute until smooth.

Bring a saucepan of water to the boil, with a steamer insert on top, and butter a 17cm/6½in pudding basin. Roll out the pastry on a lightly floured work surface into a circle about twice the size of the basin. Cut off a piece to make the lid. Gently fold the larger piece into quarters, then lower it into the basin and open it out so it lines the basin and overhangs the edges. Fill the basin with the chicken and mushrooms. Cut the remaining pastry into a circle, dampen the edges and seal to the top of the pudding by pinching the edges together. Trim off any excess. Cover the top with a circle of pleated baking paper tied with string. Steam for 2 hours until cooked through, topping up with boiling water as necessary. Leave to rest for 10–15 minutes.

Serve the suet pudding with buttered carrots.

Serves 4
Preparation time: 20 minutes, plus 30 minutes cooling, and making the stock
Cooking time: 3 hours 40 minutes

1 tbsp plain flour
600g/1lb 5oz skinless boneless chicken thighs, cut into small pieces
50g/1¾oz unsalted butter, plus extra for greasing
1 tbsp olive oil
1 large onion, finely diced
1 large garlic clove, finely diced
150g/5½oz chestnut mushrooms, halved
½ tbsp chopped thyme leaves
1 bay leaf
150ml/5fl oz/scant ⅔ cup Chicken Stock (see page 197)
sea salt and freshly ground black pepper
1 recipe quantity Buttered Carrots (see page 216), to serve

FOR THE SUET PASTRY
300g/10½oz/heaped 2⅓ cups self-raising flour, plus extra for dusting
150g/5½oz/1¼ cups suet
2 tbsp chopped Japanese red parsley or flat-leaf parsley
½ tsp mustard powder

Spiced pumpkin & chicken pithivier

A pithivier is a round, double-crust pie usually made with puff pastry, marked with a pattern on top and given a high glaze with egg wash. For this version, however, I added an element from the American pumpkin pie and came up with this mildly spicy curried filling for my puff pastry.

Melt butter in a saucepan over a medium heat. Add the onion and curry powder and fry for about 3 minutes until the onions are soft but not brown. Add the pumpkin and cook for 1–2 minutes, stirring.

Toss the chicken in the cornflour to coat, then add it to the pan with the corn and stir until combined. Add the stock and bring to a simmer, stirring occasionally, then add the cream and cook for a further 6–8 minutes until the sauce thickens and the juices run clear when the thickest part of the chicken is pierced with the tip of a sharp knife. Season with salt and pepper, cover loosely and leave to cool, then chill in the fridge for 30 minutes to firm up.

Preheat the oven to 200°C/400°F/Gas 6 and line a baking tray with baking paper. Divide the pastry in half, then roll out each piece on a lightly floured work surface to a circle about 23cm/9in and about 3mm/⅛in thick. Put one piece on the prepared baking tray and spread the cool filling over the centre of the pastry circle, leaving a 4cm/1½in gap all the way round the edge. Whisk together the egg and milk to make an egg wash, then brush the edges with egg wash. Carefully lift the other pastry circle and place it over the filled base, gently pressing out the air as you press the edges together to seal. Seal securely and make a pattern by gently pressing all the way round the edge with the tines of a fork. Use a sharp knife to score a pattern on the top of the pastry from the centre to the edges.

Brush the pastry with egg wash, then bake for 10 minutes. Turn the oven down to 150°C/300°F/Gas 2 and bake for a further 10–15 minutes until the pastry is golden. If you want a high-shine finish and a really golden colour, egg wash the pithivier a second time halfway through cooking. Serve warm with a fresh salad.

Serves 4
Preparation time: 30 minutes, plus 30 minutes chilling, and making the curry paste, stock and pastry (optional)
Cooking time: 30 minutes

50g/1¾oz unsalted butter
1 onion, finely diced
1 tbsp Curry Paste (see page 204)
300g/10½oz peeled, deseeded and diced pumpkin
2 skinless boneless chicken breasts, cut into small pieces
1 tsp cornflour
100g/3½oz/½ cup drained tinned or thawed frozen sweetcorn kernels
200ml/7fl oz/scant 1 cup Chicken Stock (see page 197)
100ml/3½fl oz/scant ½ cup double cream
600g/1lb 5oz Rough Puff Pastry (see page 208) or puff pastry, thawed if frozen
a little flour, for dusting
1 egg
1 tsp milk
sea salt and freshly ground black pepper
1 recipe quantity Green Salad (see page 219), to serve

Stilton, chicken & artichoke lasagne

Eating lasagne reminds me of growing up, as my mum always had it on the menu at our pub and I loved the rich, meaty sauce she made with the creamy béchamel. I usually precook my lasagne sheets but some just need rinsing in boiling water before assembling the lasagne, so check the instructions on the packet. I find they sometimes need a bit more liquid in the sauce, in which case, add a little stock or water.

Bring a large saucepan of lightly salted water to the boil over a high heat. Add the lasagne sheets and cook for 10 minutes until just tender, then drain and put in a bowl of ice-cold water to stop them cooking further. Drain well.

Meanwhile, heat the oil and butter in a large saucepan over a high heat. Add the onion and garlic and fry for 2 minutes until softened. Add the bacon and Jerusalem artichokes and cook for 4 minutes, stirring occasionally, then add the minced chicken and stir together for 6–8 minutes, breaking up the mince, until it is just starting to brown.

Add the puréed tomatoes, tomato purée and thyme, then the red wine sauce and bring to the boil. Turn the heat down to medium and cook for about 15 minutes until the sauce thickens slightly. Stir in the parsley and season with salt and pepper to taste, then remove from the heat.

Preheat the oven to 180°C/350°F/Gas 4 and grease an ovenproof lasagne dish. Crumble the Stilton into the béchamel sauce and warm it through to melt slightly.

Cover the bottom of the prepared dish with one-third of the meat sauce, top with a layer of lasagne sheets and cover with another one-third of the meat sauce, another layer of lasagne sheets and the last layer of meat sauce. Pour the béchamel sauce over the top and finish with the grated cheese.

Bake for about 20 minutes until the lasagne is heated through and the cheese has melted and browned slightly on top. Serve with a fresh salad and garlic bread.

Serves 4–6
Preparation time: 30 minutes, plus making the sauce
Cooking time: 50 minutes

250g/9oz lasagne sheets
1 tbsp olive oil, plus extra for greasing
30g/1oz unsalted butter
1 onion, finely diced
2 garlic cloves, finely chopped
2 smoked bacon rashers, finely diced
150g/5½oz Jerusalem artichokes, peeled and cut into small dice
600g/1lb 5oz coarsely minced chicken
200g/7oz/scant 1⅔ cups tinned chopped tomatoes, puréed
2 tbsp tomato purée
2 tbsp chopped thyme leaves
300ml/10½fl oz/scant 1¼ cups Red Wine Sauce (see page 198)
1 tbsp chopped parsley leaves
50g/1¾oz Stilton cheese, crumbled
300ml/10½fl oz/scant 1¼ cups Béchamel Sauce (see page 199)
30g/1oz Cheddar cheese, grated
sea salt and freshly ground black pepper
1 recipe quantity Green Salad (see page 219), to serve
garlic bread, to serve

Asian chicken & mushroom ballotines

Probably the best known of all the chicken flavour combinations, this simple dish really allows the ingredients to shine. A boned chicken thigh is stuffed ith forcemeat , then formed into a sausage shape and poached. I have given the dish a distinctly creamy flavour and combined that with earthy wild mushrooms and a touch of Asia with the spiced rice.

To make the stuffing, put the chicken pieces in a blender and blend until smooth. Gradually pour in the cream while pulsing the blender. Transfer the mixture to a bowl, season with salt and pepper, then cover and chill in the fridge.

Heat the butter in a large frying pan and fry the mushrooms for 5 minutes until softened. Stir in the curry paste, then leave to cool.

Combine the mushroom and chicken mixtures. Spoon into a disposable piping bag and chill for 30 minutes to firm up. Pipe the chilled mousse into each boned chicken leg, making sure it fills each one, then pull the skin over the ends to make a sausage shape.

Lay a double layer of cling film on the work surface and lay 5 slices of pancetta vertically next to each other (so there are no gaps) across the centre, then place the ballotine across the top. Fold the pancetta around the chicken until it is completely enclosed and tuck in the ends. Roll the cling film around the chicken, pushing out any air as you do so, and tie each end securely in a knot. Repeat with the remaining ballotines.

Bring a large saucepan of water to the boil over a high heat, then turn the heat down to a simmer. Add the ballotines and poach for 30 minutes until cooked through. Remove with a slotted spoon and place in a large bowl of cold water for 2–3 minutes until cool enough to handle.

Heat the oil in a large frying pan over a medium heat. Remove the ballotines from the water and take off the cling film. Add the ballotines to the pan and fry for 2–3 minutes, turning occasionally, until browned all over. Slice the ballotines, put on a bed of spiced rice and lentils and scatter with crispy fried shallots before serving.

Serves 4
Preparation time: 45 minutes, plus 30 minutes chilling, and making the curry paste
Cooking time: 40 minutes

200g/7oz chicken leg or thigh meat, cut into pieces
200ml/7fl oz/scant 1 cup double cream
2 tbsp unsalted butter
100g/3½oz wild mushrooms, such as girolles, porcini or morels, sliced
2 tbsp Curry Paste (see page 204)
4 chicken thighs, skin on, tunnel boned (see page 21)
20 thin slices of pancetta
2 tbsp olive oil
sea salt and freshly ground black pepper
1 recipe quantity Spiced Rice & Lentils (see page 210), to serve
1 recipe quantity Crispy Fried Shallots (see page 205), to serve

Medallions of chicken, peas & broad beans in tarragon cream

One of the first dishes I ever cooked was chicken breast with a cream and tarragon sauce. The flavours of tarragon, cream and chicken are just perfect together, especially when combined with the contrasting crunch of fresh peas and broad beans to make a delicious dinner at any time of the year. By cutting the chicken into medallions, it makes the recipe very quick while the chicken still remains tender.

Heat 1 tsp of the oil and the butter in a frying pan over a medium-high heat. Add the onion and garlic and fry for 1–2 minutes until softened. Add the stock and cream and simmer for 5 minutes until the liquid has reduced by half. Add the peas, beans and tarragon and stir well, then remove from the heat.

Meanwhile, put the rice in a saucepan and add enough water to come about 2cm/¾in above the rice. Bring to the boil over a high heat and cook for about 5 minutes until almost all the water has evaporated. Turn the heat down as low as it will go, cover with a lid and leave the rice to steam gently for about 5 minutes until it is tender but not soft, and is still holding its shape. Remove the pan from the heat. Keep the pan covered so the rice stays warm and leave to one side until required.

Heat the remaining oil in a large frying pan. Season the chicken with salt and pepper, then add to the pan and fry for 2–3 minutes on each side until golden and cooked through. Remove the chicken from the pan and leave to one side.

Add the sauce to the chicken frying pan and cook over a high heat for about 5 minutes until the sauce just starts to thicken slightly.

Stir the chives into the rice and season with salt and pepper to taste. Serve the chicken on top of the rice with the sauce spooned over the top.

Serves 4
Preparation time: 15 minutes, plus making the stock
Cooking time: 25 minutes

1 tbsp olive oil
1 tsp unsalted butter
1 red onion, finely diced
1 garlic clove, chopped
100ml/3½fl oz/scant ½ cup Chicken or Vegetable Stock (see page 197)
200ml/7fl oz/scant 1 cup double cream
100g/3½oz/⅔ cup podded or frozen peas, defrosted if frozen
100g/3½oz podded broad beans
2 tbsp chopped tarragon leaves
300g/10½oz/1½ cups basmati rice, rinsed
4 skinless chicken breasts, cut across into medallions
2 tbsp chopped chives
sea salt and freshly ground black pepper

Smoked chicken & wild garlic risotto

Once you master the basics of risotto, the options are endless. You can also make the base in advance, then finish it off just before serving – perfect when you are in a rush. If you can't find wild garlic, or it's out of season (spring to early summer), just use baby leaf spinach. And do have a go at smoking the chicken yourself (see page 144).

Heat the oil and butter in a large frying pan over a medium heat. Add the onion and garlic and fry for 5 minutes, stirring occasionally, until softened. Stir in the rice to coat it in the onion mixture. Pour in the wine and stir until it is absorbed by the rice.

Add a small ladleful of the hot stock and stir until the stock has been absorbed by the rice before adding the next ladleful. Keep stirring the rice to prevent it sticking and to make sure it cooks evenly. Continue adding the stock until you have used half of it; this should take about 10 minutes. This is the risotto base and it can be left at this stage, if more convenient, and the dish finished later. If you want to do this, transfer the rice to a container with a lid and leave to cool completely. When cool, cover and chill for up to 2 days.

To finish the risotto, reheat the reserved stock, if necessary. Return the rice to the large pan over a medium-low heat. Continue to add the stock a ladleful at a time as before, stirring continuously, until the stock has been absorbed and the rice is tender but still retains some bite; this will take about 10 minutes. Make sure the rice is piping hot, if reheating it.

Add the chicken, cream, Parmesan, lemon juice, wild garlic and chives. Season with salt and pepper to taste and stir until well combined and heated through. Serve the risotto sprinkled with extra Parmesan.

Serves 4
Preparation time: 20 minutes, plus making the stock
Cooking time: 35 minutes

FOR THE RISOTTO BASE

1 tbsp olive oil

75g/2½oz unsalted butter

1 large onion, finely diced

2 garlic cloves, finely diced

250g/9oz/scant 1¼ cups risotto rice, such as Arborio

200ml/7fl oz/scant 1 cup dry white wine

750ml/26fl oz/3 cups hot Vegetable Stock (see page 197)

FOR THE WILD GARLIC BUTTER

4 wild garlic leaves, finely chopped

2 wild garlic bulbs, finely chopped

125g/4½oz unsalted butter

FOR THE SMOKED CHICKEN RISOTTO

4 smoked chicken breasts (see page 144), skin-on, or roasted chicken breasts (see page 23), skinned, boned and shredded

100ml/3½fl oz/scant ½ cup double cream

150g/5½oz Parmesan cheese, grated, plus extra for serving

juice of ½ lemon

50g/1¾oz wild garlic leaves or baby spinach leaves, roughly chopped

1 tbsp chopped chives

sea salt and freshly ground black pepper

Malaysian chicken rendang

This dish is bursting with the traditional Thai flavours of chilli, fresh ginger, lemongrass and coconut milk. In my new version, you make a paste from the flavouring ingredients, then cook the meat slowly to intensify the flavours.

Preheat the oven to 160°C/315°F/Gas 2½. Put all the paste ingredients in a blender, season with salt and pepper and blitz together to a paste.

Heat the oil in a flameproof casserole dish over a medium heat, add the chicken and fry for a few minutes until lightly brown. Add the spice paste, bring to the boil, then cover with a lid, transfer to the oven and bake for 1½ hours until cooked through and completely tender.

Scatter with the coriander and serve with boiled rice.

Serves 4
Preparation time: 15 minutes
Cooking time: 1½ hours

1 tbsp olive oil
4 chicken thighs, skin on
4 chicken drumsticks, skin on
2 tbsp chopped coriander leaves
sea salt and freshly ground black pepper
boiled rice, to serve

FOR THE CURRY PASTE
1½ onions, quartered
1 tbsp ground coriander
2 lemongrass stalks, finely chopped
4 red chillies, deseeded and chopped
1 tbsp ground cumin
1 tbsp dark soft brown sugar
2 tbsp peeled and grated root ginger
3 garlic cloves
400ml/14fl oz/generous 1½ cups
   coconut milk
1 tsp Thai fish sauce
1 star anise, ground to a fine powder

Chicken rogan josh with fenugreek potatoes

Homemade curry is rather special but can take a bit of time, so I've used a curry paste that you can keep in the fridge to make things a bit easier when you want a quick meal. Rogan josh has a lovely rich tomato sauce with bags of flavour.

Heat 1 tablespoon of the oil and the butter in a large saucepan over a high heat. Add the chicken and fry for 3 minutes on each side until sealed. Remove from the pan and leave to one side until required.

Heat the remaining oil in the same pan over a low heat. Add the onions and garlic and fry for 8 minutes until softened and just starting to colour. Add the cardamom pods, cinnamon stick and curry paste and stir well, then stir in the tomatoes, tomato purée, sugar and stock. Turn the heat up to high and bring to the boil, then turn the heat down to low, cover with a lid and simmer for 1–1½ hours until the chicken is tender and almost falling apart.

When the chicken is almost ready, heat the oil and butter for the potatoes in a frying pan over a medium-high heat. Add the potatoes, sprinkle with the fenugreek seeds and stir together for a few minutes until hot.

Sprinkle the curry with the coriander and serve with the fenugreek potatoes and an onion and mint salad.

Serves 4
Preparation time: 20 minutes, plus
 making the curry paste and stock
Cooking time: 1¾ hours

3 tbsp olive oil

1 tbsp unsalted butter

8 skinless boneless chicken thighs

2 onions, finely sliced

2 garlic cloves, finely diced

2 black cardamom pods

1 cinnamon stick

4 tbsp Curry Paste (see page 204)

200g/7oz/scant 1⅔ cups tinned chopped
 tomatoes

5 tbsp tomato purée

1 tsp dark soft brown sugar

400ml/14fl oz/generous 1½ cups Chicken
 Stock (see page 197)

1–2 tbsp coriander leaves

sliced onion and mint salad, to serve

FOR THE FENUGREEK POTATOES
1 tbsp olive oil
1 tbsp unsalted butter
200g/7oz cooked new potatoes
2 tsp ground fenugreek seeds

Persian chicken

Persian cooking is about zingy flavours, often combining sweet and savoury in the traditional Middle Eastern style, with lots of citrus tang. You'll find sumac with the spices in major supermarkets or in ethnic stores – it adds to the citrus notes in this dish.

Preheat the oven to 160°C/315°F/Gas 2½ and have ready a large ovenproof dish. Put the saffron strands in a bowl, pour over 2 tablespoons hot water and leave to stand.

Heat 1 tablespoon of the clarified butter in a large frying pan over a medium-high heat. Add the chicken in two batches and fry each batch for 10 minutes until all sides are caramelized and nicely coloured. Remove the chicken from the pan and leave to one side.

Heat the remaining clarified butter and fry the cardamom pods, cinnamon, cloves and bay leaves for 1 minute until fragrant. Add the onions, season with salt and pepper and cook over a low heat for 5–10 minutes, stirring occasionally, until they start to caramelize.

Stir in the rice, dates, raisins, almonds and pistachios and ensure they are all mixed together thoroughly. Stir in 650ml/22fl oz/generous 2½ cups water, the orange, lemon and lime zest and the sumac and bring to a simmer.

Tip the rice mixture into an ovenproof dish, drizzle over the saffron water and bury the chicken thighs in the rice. Cover with kitchen foil and bake for 20–25 minutes until the water has evaporated, the rice is tender and the chicken juices run clear when the thickest part of the chicken is pierced with the tip of a sharp knife. Sprinkle with the coriander and serve.

Serves 4
Preparation time: 15 minutes,
  plus making the butter
Cooking time: 50 minutes

a good pinch of saffron strands
4 tbsp Clarified Butter (see page 196)
12 boneless chicken thighs, skin on
12 cardamom pods, crushed
2 large cinnamon sticks
4 cloves
2 dried bay leaves
2 onions, finely sliced
300g/10oz/1½ cups basmati rice, rinsed
10 dates, pitted and sliced
2 tbsp raisins
2 tbsp toasted flaked almonds
2 tbsp shelled pistachios
2 strips of orange zest
2 strips of lemon zest
2 strips of lime zest
2 tbsp sumac
2 tbsp coriander leaves
sea salt and freshly ground black pepper

Chicken bourguignon

A take on comfort food at its best, this classic dish is cooked slowly so the meat is bathed in a rich sauce flavoured with smoked bacon and mushrooms. Serve it with plenty of creamy mashed potatoes and you can't beat it.

Preheat the oven to 180°C/350°F/Gas 4. Heat 2 tablespoons oil in a large frying pan. Add the chicken, in batches if necessary, and fry for about 6 minutes until sealed on all sides, then transfer to a casserole dish, keeping the frying pan to one side.

Put the red wine, sugar and star anise in a saucepan over a high heat, bring to the boil, then boil for about 5 minutes until reduced by half.

Put the frying pan back on the heat, add the celery, onion, garlic, leek and thyme and fry for 2–3 minutes until softened and lightly browned, then add to the casserole dish with the meat.

Pour the reduced wine into the frying pan and add the stock. Bring to the boil and deglaze the pan by stirring to remove any caramelized bits stuck to the bottom. Pour into the casserole dish, cover with a lid and transfer to the oven for 1½ hours until the meat is just falling apart.

While the chicken is cooking, bring a large saucepan of water to the boil over a high heat, add the baby onions and boil for 5 minutes until softened, then remove from the water with a slotted spoon, plunge into ice-cold water, then drain and leave to one side. Return the water to the boil, add the carrots and boil for 2 minutes, then remove from the pan, plunge into the ice-cold water, drain and add to the onions. Heat 1 teaspoon oil in a frying pan and fry the bacon until crisp, then dice and add to the onions. Stir the mushrooms into the pan and fry for 5 minutes until softened, then add to the onions.

When the chicken is cooked, stir in the onion mixture and the parsley, then bake for a further 10 minutes. Serve with creamy mashed potatoes.

Serves 4
Preparation time: 1 hour, plus making the stock
Cooking time: 2 hours

2 tbsp plus 1 tsp olive oil
12 skinless boneless chicken thighs, cut in half
1 bottle of dry red wine
1 tbsp dark soft brown sugar
1 star anise
1 celery stick, finely diced
1 onion, finely diced
2 garlic cloves, finely chopped
1 leek, trimmed and finely sliced
1 thyme sprig
500ml/17fl oz/2 cups Chicken Stock (see page 197)
16 baby onions or shallots
2 carrots, peeled and diced
1 tsp olive oil
2 smoked bacon rashers
100g/3½oz chestnut mushrooms, quartered
1 tbsp chopped parsley leaves
1 recipe quantity Creamy Mashed Potatoes (see page 212), to serve

Spinach-rolled chicken with onion purée & charred leeks

Rinse and drain the spinach, then put it in a saucepan with just the water clinging to the leaves. Put over a medium heat until softened, then drain.

Put one chicken breast in between two sheets of baking paper and gently beat to flatten. Lay a double layer of cling film on the work surface, put the flat chicken breast on top, season with salt and pepper and top with some spinach. Roll the chicken breast to encase the filling, then roll the cling film around the whole thing, pushing out any air, and tie each end securely in a knot. Wrap in the same way with kitchen foil. Repeat with the remaining chicken.

Bring a saucepan of water to the boil over a high heat, then turn the heat down to low, add the chicken and simmer for 30 minutes until the juices run clear when the thickest part of the chicken is pierced with the tip of a sharp knife.

Meanwhile, to make the onion purée, heat the butter in a large saucepan over a medium heat, add the onions and fry for about 20 minutes until softened and golden. Season with salt and pepper. Put into a blender and blitz to a purée, adding a little boiling water if the purée is too thick.

At the same time, bring a saucepan of water to the boil over a high heat, add the baby leeks and cook for 1 minute, then drain and put in a bowl of ice-cold water for 5 minutes. Drain and pat dry.

Put the leeks in a bowl and drizzle with 1 tablespoon of the oil. Heat a griddle pan over a high heat, add the leeks and cook until they have charred black markings.

Remove the cooked chicken from the water and leave to rest for 2 minutes before unwrappping. Heat the remaining oil in a frying pan, add the chicken and fry on all sides until golden. Slice the chicken into medallions and put on top of the warm onion purée with the charred leeks. Serve with potato croquettes and wilted greens.

Serves 4
Preparation time: 40 minutes
Cooking time: 40 minutes

200g/7oz spinach leaves
4 skinless chicken breasts
50g/1¾oz unsalted butter
300g/10½oz onions or shallots, finely sliced
12 baby leeks, trimmed
2 tbsp olive oil
sea salt and freshly ground black pepper
1 recipe quantity Potato Croquettes (see page 214), to serve
1 recipe quantity Wilted Greens (see page 217), to serve

Chicken supremes in lovage butter en papillote

Cooking en papillote – or in a parcel – is a fantastic way of preparing chicken. It steams all the ingredients together and keeps the chicken lovely and moist, then once the vegetables are cooked, they reduce down and make a juicy broth. Serve these on a plate or boards, still in the paper, so your guests can open their parcel themselves and get the first whiff of the fresh vegetables and herbs with the golden chicken.

Preheat the oven to 180°C/350°F/Gas 4. Put the potatoes in a saucepan of water, cover and bring to the boil over a high heat. Turn the heat down to medium and cook for 10 minutes until tender, then drain and leave to one side.

Season the chicken with salt and pepper. Heat 1 tablespoon of the oil in a frying pan over a medium heat, add the chicken and fry for a few minutes until just coloured on all sides, then remove from the heat.

Mix together the butter, lovage, tarragon and garlic.

Put four large sheets of baking paper on the work surface. Divide the samphire, peas, courgettes and tomatoes among the papers, then top each pile with a tablespoon of the herb butter. Put a chicken supreme on top of the vegetables and a teaspoon of butter on top. Season with a little salt and pepper. Bring the edges of the baking paper up over the ingredients of the first parcel and fold and scrunch the edges together to seal. Repeat to form 3 more parcels and put them in a roasting tin.

Bake the parcels for 15–20 minutes, then carefully open one to check that the juices run clear when the thickest part of the chicken is pierced with the tip of a sharp knife.

Meanwhile, heat the remaining oil in a frying pan over a high heat. Add the chorizo and fry for a few minutes until browned, then add the potatoes and stir until heated through. Serve the chicken still in the paper so your guests can open their own parcel, with the potatoes and chorizo.

Serves 4
Preparation time: 20 minutes
Cooking time: 30 minutes

20 baby new potatoes
4 chicken supremes, skin on
3 tbsp olive oil
125g/4½oz salted butter, softened
3 tbsp chopped lovage or watercress
1 tsp chopped tarragon leaves
2 garlic cloves, crushed
120g/4¼oz samphire grass
60g/2¼oz/heaped ⅓ cup podded peas
2 courgettes, roughly diced
2 large vine tomatoes, chopped, including seeds
55g/2oz chorizo, finely sliced
sea salt and freshly ground black pepper

Chicken with fig & goats' cheese wrapped in Parma ham

This is such a simple recipe but so effective and delicious that it can take centre stage at your next dinner party for friends. The stuffing and the Parma ham wrap both help to keep the meat beautifully moist as well as imparting plenty of flavour.

Preheat the oven to 200°C/400°F/Gas 6. Make a horizontal slit down each chicken breast, making sure you don't cut right through. Open up the chicken breasts as flat as possible and place each one on 2 strips of Parma ham.

Mix together the figs and goats' cheese, then put one-quarter of the mixture on each chicken breast and season with salt and pepper. Fold the chicken over the filling, then wrap the ham around the outside and secure with cocktail sticks, if necessary.

Heat the oil in a frying pan, add the chicken breasts and cook for 2 minutes on each side until browned, then transfer to a roasting tin and roast for 15 minutes until the juices run clear when the thickest part of the chicken is pierced with the tip of a sharp knife.

Serve hot with a fresh salad and buttered new potatoes.

Serves 4
Preparation time: 15 minutes
Cooking time: 20 minutes

4 skinless chicken breasts
8 strips of Parma ham
8 fresh figs, sliced
100g/3½oz soft goats' cheese, crumbled
1 tbsp olive oil
sea salt and freshly ground black pepper
1 recipe quantity Green Salad (see page 219) or a mixed leaf salad, to serve
boiled and buttered new potatoes, to serve

Asian-style chicken Kiev

I'm sure everyone at some point has eaten a chicken Kiev, a classic combination of chicken rolled or stuffed with garlic butter and herbs, then breaded and fried or baked in the oven. There is dispute as to whether it was created in Russia, in Paris, or actually in Kiev, the capital of the Ukraine, but it certainly gained popularity in the 1970s and became a classic recipe for pub, restaurant and supermarket ready-meals in the UK and elsewhere. But giving it an Asian twist changes the style and brings it right up to date, lifting the rather predictable flavours to give a fantastic, pungent and spicy chicken dish.

Beat the softened butter in a mixing bowl for 30 seconds. Mix in the lime zest and juice, the mint, coriander, garlic and ginger, and season with salt and pepper. Mix thoroughly, then cover and chill in the fridge for about an hour, if you can, for the flavours to develop. Remove from the fridge to soften just before you are ready to use it.

Using a small, very sharp knife, make a slit in the flesh of each breast fillet from top to bottom, creating a pocket at a slight angle. Spoon the butter mixture into a piping bag with a large plain nozzle and pipe into the pocket.

Put the cornflour in a shallow bowl and season with salt and pepper. Tip the beaten eggs into another shallow bowl and the breadcrumbs into a third. Toss the stuffed chicken breasts first in the flour to coat, shaking off any excess, then slide them one at a time into the egg and turn until covered. Finally, dip each one into the breadcrumbs, again shaking off any excess. Lay the breasts, slit sides down, on a plate, cover and chill in the fridge for at least 30 minutes to help firm the crumb coating.

When ready to cook, preheat the oven to 190°C/375°F/ Gas 5. Heat the oil in an ovenproof frying pan over a medium heat until you can feel a good heat rising. Add the chicken breasts and fry for 1–2 minutes on each side until lightly golden. Transfer the pan to the oven and cook for 12–14 minutes until golden brown and the juices run clear when the thickest part of the chicken is pierced with the tip of a sharp knife. Spoon over any butter from the roasting pan and serve hot with roast potatoes and green beans.

Serves 4
Preparation time: 25 minutes,
  plus 1½ hours chilling
Cooking time: 16 minutes

200g/7oz unsalted butter, softened
grated zest and juice of 1 lime
leaves from 6 mint sprigs, roughly
  chopped
2 handfuls of coriander leaves and stalks
3 large garlic cloves, finely chopped
5cm/2.5in piece of root ginger, peeled
  and finely chopped
4 skinless chicken breasts
100g/3½oz/heaped ¾ cup cornflour
2 large eggs, beaten
100g/3½oz/1 cup panko breadcrumbs
3 tbsp sunflower oil
sea salt and freshly ground black pepper
1 recipe quantity Roast Potatoes
  (see page 212), to serve
steamed green beans, to serve

Chargrilled chicken tikka on lemongrass sticks

Chicken tikka is one of our most popular dishes and when you use lemongrass as the kebab skewers, you get another layer of flavour coming into the mix. If you don't have any, though, you can simply use ordinary metal or soaked wooden skewers.

Mix together all the marinade ingredients in a non-metallic baking tray. Thread the chicken onto the lemongrass stalks and put in the tray, turning to coat the meat. Cover with cling film and leave to marinate in the fridge for 2 hours.

Meanwhile, mix the onion, chicory leaves and tomatoes in a bowl. Whisk together the lemon juice and oil, then drizzle over the salad, cover with cling film and chill in the fridge until ready to serve.

Preheat the barbecue or a large griddle pan and cook the chicken for about 10 minutes, turning frequently, until the juices run clear when the thickest part of the chicken is pierced with the tip of a sharp knife.

Serve the chicken with the onion and tomato salsa and some naan bread.

Serves 4
Preparation time: 20 minutes,
  plus 2 hours marinating
Cooking time: 10 minutes

1kg/2lb 4oz skinless boneless chicken
  thighs, cut into cubes
8 lemongrass stalks
1 red onion, thinly sliced
4 chicory heads, separated into leaves
4 large vine tomatoes, quartered
juice of ½ lemon
1 tbsp olive oil
naan bread, to serve

FOR THE MARINADE
100g/3½oz/scant ½ cup natural yogurt
1 tsp peeled and grated root ginger
2 garlic cloves, grated
1 tsp mild Madras curry powder
1 tsp garam masala
1 tsp lemon juice
1 tbsp tomato purée
2 tsp caster sugar
½ tsp chilli powder

Golden chicken & mint mojito

A mojito is a classic cocktail – fresh mint from the garden with sharp lime and white rum sweetened with sugar syrup. The combination was too perfect not to use for a recipe as it brings all those elements to lift the chicken, so here is my mojito chicken, using golden rum instead of white for a simple but effective twist. I love this dish cooked on the barbecue for that smoked, charred flavour or, if you are in the kitchen, use a griddle pan for a similar effect.

Score the chicken breasts a couple of times across the top and bottom to allow the marinade to penetrate. Put the rum, lime zest and juice, mint, ginger, coriander and sugar into a small blender or pestle and mortar and crush to a paste. Rub the marinade into the chicken, put in a non-metallic bowl, cover and leave to marinate in the fridge for at least 2 hours or overnight if possible.

If you are using a barbecue, wait for the charcoal to go white with no naked flames, then cook the chicken breasts for 2–3 minutes on each side, then keep turning them and brushing with marinade for a further 5–10 minutes until the juices from the chicken run clear when the thickest part of the chicken is pierced with the tip of a sharp knife. Baste with plenty of marinade while they are cooking so they don't dry out.

If you are in the kitchen, preheat the oven to 200°C/400°F/Gas 6. Heat a griddle pan over a high heat until very hot, then add the chicken breasts and seal for 2 minutes on each side until you have charred stripes on the meat. Transfer to the oven and cook for 5 minutes until cooked through and tender. Slice the chicken, scatter with mint leaves and lime wedges and serve with a fresh, crisp salad and new potatoes.

Serves 4
Preparation time: 10 minutes, plus overnight marinating
Cooking time: 20 minutes

4 skinless chicken breasts
6 tbsp golden rum
grated zest and juice of 2 limes
leaves from 12 large mint sprigs, plus extra to serve
1cm/$\frac{1}{2}$in piece of root ginger, peeled and chopped
12 large coriander sprigs, including stalks
2 tbsp dark soft brown sugar
2 limes, cut into wedges
1 recipe quantity Green Salad (see page 219), to serve
boiled new potatoes, to serve

Barbecued garlic & thyme spatchcock poussin with celeriac, beetroot & sunflower seed coleslaw

If you are feeling very confident with a knife, you can cut the celeriac and beetroot into very fine matchstick shapes. And don't be put off by the idea of spatchcocking the poussins – it is really very simple and makes for a dramatic presentation.

Beat together the butter, garlic and thyme until well blended. Rub into the poussins, pushing some under the skin of the breast if you can to help keep the meat moist when cooking. Preheat the barbecue or oven to maximum.

To make the coleslaw, put the celeriac and beetroot in a bowl and stir in the lemon juice. Add the mayonnaise, crème fraîche, mustards and parsley and mix well. Add the toasted sunflower seeds and season with salt and pepper to taste. Cover and put in the fridge until required.

Cook the poussins over maximum heat on the barbecue for 1–2 minutes on each side, then transfer to a higher shelf and cook with the lid closed for another 5–10 minutes until the juices run clear when the thickest part of the chicken is pierced with the tip of a sharp knife. Alternatively, cook in the oven for 4 minutes, then turn the oven temperature down to 190°C/375°F/Gas 5 and cook for a further 10 minutes. Leave to rest for a couple of minutes in a warm place, then serve hot with the coleslaw.

Serves 4
Preparation time: 30 minutes, plus making the mayonnaise
Cooking time: 15 minutes

4 tbsp unsalted butter
2 garlic cloves, finely diced
leaves from 2 thyme sprigs, chopped
4 poussins, spatchcocked (see page 20)
½ celeriac, peeled and grated
2 beetroot, peeled and grated
2 tsp freshly squeezed lemon juice
4 tbsp Mayonnaise (see page 202)
2 tbsp crème fraîche
2 tbsp Dijon mustard
2 tsp wholegrain mustard
2 tsp chopped parsley leaves
2 tbsp sunflower seeds, lightly toasted
sea salt and freshly ground black pepper

Maple & mustard-glazed poussins with spring onion & lemon couscous

The great thing about poussins is that you can cook them on the bone so they stay lovely and moist and, of course, they are perfect for one person. This maple and mustard glaze makes the poussins sweet and sticky, counterbalanced by the citrus couscous.

Preheat the oven to 180°C/350°F/Gas 4. Mix together the maple syrup, mustard, soy sauce and orange juice. Peel 4 of the garlic cloves and put a garlic clove and a thyme sprig inside each of the poussins, then tie the legs together and put them in a roasting tin. Pour over the maple syrup mixture and stir in the remaining garlic. Roast for about 20–25 minutes, basting occasionally with the syrup, until the poussins are cooked through and the juices run clear when a knife is inserted into the thigh.

Meanwhile, bring the stock to the boil in a saucepan over a high heat. Put the couscous in a bowl and pour over the stock, stirring continuously. Cover with cling film and leave for 15–20 minutes until the couscous is tender and has absorbed most of the liquid. Drain off any excess liquid. Stir in the spring onions, chives and lemon zest and juice, and season with salt and pepper to taste.

Leave the poussins to rest for 3–4 minutes, then serve on a bed of lemon couscous.

Serves 4
Preparation time: 15 minutes, and making the stock
Cooking time: 25 minutes

150ml/5fl oz/scant ⅔ cup maple syrup
4 tbsp wholegrain mustard
2 tbsp light soy sauce
2 tbsp freshly squeezed orange juice
12 unpeeled garlic cloves, flattened with a knife
4 thyme sprigs
4 poussins
250ml/9fl oz/1 cup Chicken Stock (see page 197)
250g/9oz/1⅓ cups couscous
6 spring onions, finely sliced
2 tbsp chopped chives
grated zest and juice of 1 lemon
sea salt and freshly ground black pepper

basic recipes

Clarified butter or ghee

Melt the butter in a saucepan over a low heat. Alternatively, put it in a clear microwave container and melt in the microwave.

Remove from the heat and leave to settle, then gently pour off the clear butter into a jug, making sure you leave behind the white fats floating on the top or settled at the bottom.

Store in an airtight container in the fridge for up to a week.

Makes 250g/9oz
Preparation time: 2 minutes, plus settling
Cooking time: 2 minutes

250g/9oz unsalted butter

Herb oil

Bring a saucepan of water to the boil over a high heat and have a bowl of ice-cold water ready. Add the herbs and spinach to the boiling water and blanch for 1 minute, then lift out with a slotted spoon and put into the ice-cold water to stop them cooking any further.

Lift the herbs and spinach out of the ice-cold water and gently shake off any excess, then transfer to a small blender. Add the oil and blitz to a purée, then season with salt and pepper to taste. Put in an airtight container and leave to infuse in the fridge overnight.

Secure a muslin cloth over the top of a jug. Pour the oil into the jug through the muslin, then leave it to one side to strain for a few hours, without disturbing it. Discard the solids and pour the clear oil into an airtight container.

Store in an airtight container in the fridge for up to a week.

Makes about 200ml/7fl oz/scant 1 cup
Preparation time: 15 minutes, plus 3 hours straining and overnight infusing
Cooking time: 1 minute

1 tsp chopped basil leaves
1 tsp chopped chives
2 tsp chopped flat-leaf parsley leaves
80g/2¾oz spinach leaves
250ml/9fl oz/2 cups olive oil
sea salt and freshly ground black pepper

Chicken stock

Preheat the oven to 200°C/400°F/Gas 6. Put the carcases in a roasting tin and roast for 1 hour until browned.

Transfer to a large saucepan and add all the remaining ingredients and 3l/105fl oz/12 cups cold water. Bring to the boil over a high heat, then turn the heat down as low as possible and simmer gently for 1–2 hours, skimming occasionally to remove any scum floating to the top.

Remove from the heat, cover and leave to cool for a couple of hours. Strain into a clean pan, discarding the bones and vegetables. Bring to the boil, then boil until reduced to about 1l/35fl oz/4 cups of stock.

Store in an airtight container in the fridge for up to 4 days or freeze in conveniently sized containers.

Makes 1l/35fl oz/4 cups
Preparation time: 10 minutes, plus 2 hours cooling
Cooking time: 3½ hours

2.5kg/5lb chicken carcases
2 unpeeled onions, quartered
4 carrots, broken in half
1 garlic bulb, cut in half horizontally
2 leeks, trimmed and halved
2 celery sticks
2 thyme sprigs
2 small bunches of flat-leaf parsley
2 bay leaves
12 black peppercorns
6 vine tomatoes
2 star anise

Vegetable stock

Put all the ingredients in a large saucepan over a high heat and add 2l/70fl oz/8 cups cold water. Bring to the boil, then turn the heat down to low and simmer for 30 minutes.

Pour the contents of the saucepan into a plastic container, cool, then store in the fridge overnight.

Strain the stock and discard any solids. Store in an airtight container in the fridge for up to a week or freeze in conveniently sized containers.

Makes 2l/70fl oz/8 cups
Preparation time: 10 minutes, plus overnight chilling
Cooking time: 40 minutes

3 onions, quartered
4 carrots, chopped
2 leeks, trimmed and chopped
2 celery sticks, chopped
1 garlic bulb, cut in half horizontally
12 black peppercorns
2 star anise
2 tarragon sprigs
2 thyme sprigs
2 parsley sprigs
1 rosemary sprig
1 sage sprig
1 lovage sprig (optional)
80g/2¾oz dried wild mushrooms
200ml/7fl oz/scant 1 cup white wine

Red wine sauce

Heat the oil in a large saucepan over a medium heat.
Add the vegetables and thyme and fry for 4–5 minutes.

Add the wine and port and deglaze the pan by stirring to
remove any caramelized bits stuck to the bottom. Bring
to the boil, then simmer to reduce the liquid by half.

Add the stock, redcurrant jelly and star anise, return to the
boil, then simmer for about 30–40 minutes until the liquid
has been reduced by about half.

Pass the liquid through a fine sieve, then season with salt
and pepper to taste. If you want the sauce to be thicker, put
the strained liquid back on the heat and bring to the boil
and reduce further until it reaches the desired thickness.

Store in an airtight container in the fridge for up to 4 days
or freeze in conveniently sized containers for up to
a month.

Makes about 750ml/26fl oz/3 cups
Preparation time: 20 minutes, plus
  making the stock
Cooking time: 1 hour

2 tbsp olive oil
1 celery stick, diced
1 leek, trimmed and finely sliced
1 carrot, peeled and diced
1 onion, finely diced
2 thyme sprigs
350ml/12fl oz/scant 1½ cups dry red wine
100ml/3½fl oz/scant ½ cup port
1.5l/52fl oz/6 cups Chicken Stock
  (see page 197)
100g/3½oz redcurrant jelly
1 star anise
sea salt and freshly ground black pepper

Traditional chicken gravy

After you have roasted the chicken, remove it from the
roasting tin, cover and leave in a warm place while you
make the gravy.

Put the roasting tin over a medium-high heat and bring
the juices to the boil. Whisk in the flour and cook for
1–2 minutes, whisking or stirring continuously, until
thickened. Whisk in the port and stock, then the sugar
and bring to the boil.

Deglaze the tin by stirring to remove any caramelized
bits stuck to the bottom. Season with salt and pepper to
taste. Cook for about 5–10 minutes until thick, then strain
through a sieve and serve hot.

Makes about 400ml/14fl oz/1½ cups
Preparation time: 5 minutes, plus
  making the stock
Cooking time: 15 minutes

meat juices from roasting a chicken
30g/1oz/¼ cup plain flour
55ml/1¾fl oz/scant ¼ cup port
500ml/17fl oz/2 cups Chicken Stock
  (see page 197)
1 tsp dark soft brown sugar
sea salt and freshly ground black pepper

Béchamel sauce

Melt the butter in a non-stick saucepan over a low heat.
Mix in the flour, using a wooden spoon, and slowly beat
together for a few minutes. Remove the pan from the heat
and whisk in the milk until blended.

Return to a medium heat, add the studded onion and
bring just to the boil, stirring continuously. Turn the heat
down to low and simmer for about 20 minutes, stirring
occasionally to make sure the sauce doesn't stick to the
bottom of the pan.

Remove from the heat and strain through a sieve into a
clean bowl. Cover with a circle of baking paper to fit the
top of the sauce to stop a skin forming. Leave to cool.

Store in an airtight container in the fridge for up to 2 days.

Makes 500ml/17fl oz/2 cups
Preparation time: 10 minutes
Cooking time: 25 minutes

50g/1¾oz unsalted butter
50g/1¾oz/heaped ⅓ cup plain flour
500ml/17 fl oz/2 cups warm milk
1 onion studded with 15 cloves

Tomato sauce

Melt the butter in a saucepan over a medium heat. Add
the onion and celery and fry for 2 minutes. Add all the
remaining ingredients and bring to the boil.

Turn the heat down to low and simmer for about 1 hour
until rich and thick. Remove and discard the herbs, then
leave to cool.

Store in an airtight container in the fridge for up to a week.

Makes 600ml/21fl oz/scant 2½ cups
Preparation time: 10 minutes, plus
making the stock
Cooking time: 1¼ hours

50g/1¾oz unsalted butter
1 onion, finely diced
1 celery stick, finely chopped
1 garlic clove, finely chopped
3 tbsp tomato purée
400g/14oz/scant 1⅔ cups tinned chopped
tomatoes
1 thyme sprig
1 rosemary sprig
300ml/10½fl oz/scant 1¼ cups Chicken
or Vegetable Stock (see page 197)
1 bay leaf

Sweet & sour sauce

Heat the groundnut oil in a small saucepan over a medium heat. Add the garlic, chilli, ginger and pepper and fry for 2–3 minutes until softened and fragrant. Add the pineapple juice, sugar, ketchup, vinegar, soy sauce and salt. Bring to the boil, then turn the heat down to low and simmer for a few minutes, stirring continuously, until the ingredients are well blended and the sugar has dissolved.

In a small bowl, mix the cornflour to a paste with 4 tablespoons water, then stir it into the sauce, bring it back to a simmer and cook for 1 minute, stirring, until the sauce has thickened. Finally add the sesame oil and stir it into the sauce until blended.

Store in an airtight container in the fridge for up to 3 days.

Makes about 310ml/10¾fl oz/1¼ cups
Preparation time: 5 minutes
Cooking time: 10 minutes

2 tbsp groundnut oil
2 garlic cloves, roughly chopped
½ red chilli with seeds, roughly chopped
1cm/½in piece of root ginger, peeled and
  roughly chopped
2 tbsp finely diced red pepper
4 tbsp pineapple juice
4 tbsp caster sugar
2 tbsp tomato ketchup
2 tbsp white wine vinegar
1 tbsp soy sauce
a pinch of salt
1½ tsp cornflour
1 tbsp sesame oil

Hoisin sauce

Put all the ingredients in a large, non-metallic bowl. Whisk them together until well blended.

Store in an airtight container in the fridge for up to 4 days.

Serves 4
Preparation time: 5 minutes

4 tbsp dark soy sauce
2 tbsp miso paste
1 tbsp molasses or clear honey
1 garlic clove, finely diced
2 tsp sesame oil
1 tsp Chinese hot sauce
2 tsp rice vinegar
½ tsp freshly ground black pepper
1 tbsp sesame seeds
1 tbsp oyster sauce

Fresh basil or rocket pesto

Grind the basil or rocket, Parmesan, garlic and nuts to a paste in a small blender or with a pestle and mortar. Gradually beat in the oil until you have a smooth paste. Season with salt and pepper to taste.

Store in an airtight container in the fridge for up to 2 days.

Makes 250ml/9fl oz/1 cup
Preparation time: 10 minutes

60g/2¼oz basil leaves or rocket leaves
25g/1oz Parmesan cheese, grated
1 garlic clove
1 tbsp pine nuts, hazelnuts or walnuts
125–150ml/4–5fl oz/½–scant ⅔ cup olive oil
sea salt and freshly ground black pepper

Guacamole

Cut the avocados in half, remove the pits, then scoop out the inside, using a spoon, and put into a bowl. Add the lime juice and crush with the back of a fork, then add the coriander and season with salt and pepper to taste.

Serves 4
Preparation time: 10 minutes

2 ripe avocados
juice of ½ lime
1 tbsp chopped coriander leaves
1 tbsp sea salt
1 tsp freshly ground black pepper

Tomato salsa

Put all the ingredients in a large bowl. Whisk together until well blended, then season with salt and pepper to taste.

Store in an airtight container in the fridge for up to 2 days.

Serves 4
Preparation time: 10 minutes

4 large ripe vine tomatoes with seeds, finely chopped
½ red onion, finely diced
2 spring onions, finely sliced
2 tbsp chopped coriander leaves
1 tbsp chopped chives
1 green chilli, deseeded and finely chopped
sea salt and freshly ground black pepper

Mayonnaise

Whisk together the egg yolks, mustard, vinegar and lemon juice in a non-metallic bowl until the mixture goes slightly pale and thickens. Gradually drizzle in the oil, a little at a time, whisking continuously until the mayonnaise thickens.

If the mayonnaise is too thick once all the oil has been added, whisk in 1–2 teaspoons warm water. Season with salt and pepper to taste. If you like, stir in some chopped herbs or spices, according to the recipe.

Store in an airtight container in the fridge for up to 3 days.

Makes about 300ml/10½fl oz/ scant 1¼ cups
Preparation time: 5 minutes

2 large egg yolks
1 tsp Dijon mustard
1 tbsp white wine vinegar
1 tsp lemon juice
250ml/9fl oz/1 cup rapeseed oil
sea salt and freshly ground black pepper
1 tbsp chopped herbs of your choice (optional)
1 tsp spice of your choice, such as chilli powder or nutmeg (optional)

Tartare sauce

Put all the ingredients in a non-metallic bowl and whisk together until well blended, seasoning with salt and pepper to taste.

Store in an airtight container in the fridge for up to 3 days.

Makes about 100ml/3½fl oz/scant ½ cup
Preparation time: 5 minutes, plus making the mayonnaise

6 tbsp Mayonnaise (see page 202)
2 tbsp drained capers, finely chopped
2 tbsp chopped gherkins
1 tsp chopped parsley leaves
1 tsp chopped chives
1 tsp chopped dill
1 tsp finely diced shallots
1 tsp lemon juice
sea salt and freshly ground black pepper

Bean house salad dressing

Put all the ingredients in a large, non-metallic bowl. Whisk them together until well blended, then season with salt and pepper to taste.

Store the dressing in an airtight container in the fridge for up to 2 weeks.

Makes about 500ml/17fl oz/2 cups
Preparation time: 5 minutes

320ml/11fl oz/scant 1⅓ cups olive oil
150ml/5fl oz/scant ⅔ cup white wine
  vinegar
1 tbsp Dijon mustard
1 tbsp wholegrain mustard
3 tbsp clear honey
sea salt and freshly ground black pepper

Miso dressing

Put all the ingredients in a non-metallic bowl and whisk together until well blended, seasoning with salt and pepper to taste.

Store in an airtight container in the fridge for up to 3 days.

Makes about 150ml/5fl oz/scant ⅔ cup
Preparation time: 5 minutes

4 tbsp light soy sauce
2 tbsp sesame oil
2 tbsp mirin
3–4 tbsp miso paste
4 tsp white wine vinegar
2 tsp clear honey
sea salt and freshly ground black pepper

Caesar salad dressing

Put all the ingredients in a non-metallic bowl and whisk together until well blended, seasoning with salt and pepper to taste.

Store in an airtight container in the fridge for up to 3 days.

Makes about 125ml/4fl oz/½ cup
Preparation time: 5 minutes, plus
  making the mayonnaise

½ tsp anchovy paste
1 tbsp white wine vinegar
2 tbsp Mayonnaise (see page 202)
1 tbsp Dijon mustard
½ garlic clove, crushed
¼ tsp lemon juice
3 tbsp olive oil
1 tbsp freshly grated Parmesan cheese
sea salt and freshly ground black pepper

Curry paste

Put the seeds and peppercorns in a dry frying pan over a medium heat and cook for about 3 minutes, stirring, until the mustard seeds start to pop and the seeds turn golden and aromatic. Tip into a bowl and leave to cool for a few minutes.

Put the turmeric, cinnamon, paprika and dried chilli in a pestle and mortar or spice grinder, add the toasted spices and the salt and grind together into a fine powder.

Add the ginger, garlic, tomato purée and vinegar and grind or bash to a paste.

Use straight away, or spoon the paste into a screw-topped jar, top with a little oil and seal with a lid. Keep in an airtight jar in the fridge for up to 2 weeks.

Makes 200g/7oz
Preparation time: 20 minutes
Cooking time: 5 minutes

3 tbsp coriander seeds
2 tbsp cumin seeds
1 tbsp mustard seeds
1 tsp fennel seeds
1 tsp black peppercorns
1 tsp ground turmeric
1 tsp ground cinnamon
1 tsp paprika
1 dried chilli
1 tsp salt
2.5cm/1in piece of root ginger,
    peeled and finely grated
4 garlic cloves, finely grated
1 tbsp tomato purée
4 tbsp cider vinegar
a little sunflower oil, to cover the
    paste while storing

Roasted garlic

Preheat the oven to 180°C/350°F/Gas 4. Put the garlic in a roasting tin, then drizzle with the oil and bake for 10 minutes until golden brown and tender. Leave to cool.

Store in an airtight container in the fridge for up to 2 weeks. Squeeze the garlic out of the papery skins when required.

Makes about 110g/3¾oz
Preparation time: 5 minutes
Cooking time: 10 minutes

6 garlic bulbs, cloves separated
    but not peeled
6 tbsp oil

Thai curry paste

Put all the ingredients into a small blender and blitz together to a paste, or crush in a pestle and mortar.

Store in an airtight container in the fridge for up to a week.

Makes 225g/8oz
Preparation time: 15 minutes

3 green chillies, deseeded and roughly
   chopped
3 garlic cloves, crushed
2 tbsp finely chopped or grated
   lemongrass stalks
4 shallots, finely chopped
1 tbsp peeled and grated root ginger
1 tbsp finely chopped kaffir lime leaves
2 tsp ground coriander
2 tsp ground cumin
1 tbsp Thai fish sauce
1 small bunch of coriander stalks
2 tbsp chopped spinach leaves
2 tbsp olive oil
sea salt and freshly ground black pepper

Crispy fried shallots

Heat 2cm/¾in of oil in a deep, heavy-based saucepan to 170°C/325°F, when a cube of bread browns in 60 seconds.

Dip the shallot rings into the milk and make sure all the rings have separated, then dip in the flour, shaking off any excess.

Fry in the hot oil for about 3 minutes until crisp, then drain on kitchen paper and serve hot.

Serves 4
Preparation time: 10 minutes
Cooking time: 5 minutes

groundnut oil, for frying
4 banana shallots, sliced into rings
100ml/3½fl oz/scant ½ cup milk
50g/1¾oz/heaped ⅓ cup self-raising flour

Spiced apple chutney

Put the apples, onion and 80ml/2½fl oz/⅓ cup water in a saucepan over a medium heat and bring to the boil. Turn the heat down to low and simmer for 15 minutes until the onion is soft.

Add the salt, spices and half the vinegar and continue to simmer for 10 minutes, stirring occasionally. Add the sugar, syrup and the remaining vinegar and simmer for a further 5 minutes, stirring, until thick and fragrant.

Spoon into airtight jars and keep for up to 2 months unopened. Once opened, refrigerate and use within 2–3 weeks.

Makes about 1kg/2lb 4oz
Preparation time: 20 minutes
Cooking time: 35 minutes

750g/1lb 10oz cooking apples, peeled, cored and finely chopped
250g/9oz onion, diced
2 tsp sea salt
2 tsp ground ginger
½ tbsp ground cinnamon
¼ tsp cayenne pepper
270ml/9½fl oz/generous 1 cup white wine vinegar
250g/9oz/1⅓ cups dark soft brown sugar
125g/4½oz golden syrup

Mango chutney

Bring all the ingredients to the boil in a large saucepan over a medium heat, then turn the heat down to low and leave to simmer for 15–20 minutes, stirring occasionally, until rich and thick. Leave to cool slightly.

Spoon into airtight jars and leave to finish cooling. Seal with the lids and keep in the fridge. It will keep for several weeks.

Makes about 600g/1lb 5oz
Preparation time: 15 minutes
Cooking time: 25 minutes

2 ripe mangoes, peeled, pitted and cut into chunks
2.5cm/1in piece of root ginger, peeled and chopped
1 garlic clove, crushed
½ tsp mustard seeds
½ tsp cumin seeds
¼ red chilli, deseeded and finely chopped
1½ tbsp white wine vinegar
1½ tbsp caster sugar

Fresh egg pasta

Put the flour in a bowl and make a well in the centre. Pour the eggs into the well. Gradually whisk the flour into the eggs, a little at a time, then add the oil and start to mix the ingredients together with your hands until you have a soft dough.

Knead and pull the dough for about 3 minutes on a lightly floured surface. Lightly oil a bowl, add the dough, then cover with cling film and chill in the fridge for at least 30 minutes.

Roll out the dough to about 0.5mm on a floured surface or use a pasta machine. Use to make ravioli, tagliatelli, linguine or other pasta shapes.

Makes 500g/1lb 2oz
Preparation time: 15 minutes, plus 30 minutes resting

400g/14oz/heaped 3½ cups pasta flour, plus extra for dusting
4 eggs, beaten with a pinch of salt
1 tbsp olive oil, plus extra for greasing

Pizza dough

Mix together the flour and salt in a bowl. In another bowl, add the yeast to 325ml/11fl oz/scant 1⅓ cups warm water, leave for 1 minute, then stir until dissolved. Pour into the flour and bring together to a smooth, slightly tacky dough.

Turn the dough onto a lightly floured work surface and knead for about 2 minutes until the dough is smooth and no longer sticky.

Put the dough in an oiled bowl, cover with cling film and leave in a warm, not hot, place for 1 hour to prove.

Turn the dough out onto a lightly floured work surface, knock the air out of the dough by punching it with your fist and knead again for a few minutes.

Use as directed in the recipe or split and roll the dough into pizza bases. For a thin base, roll as thinly as you can, put on a baking tray, add the topping and bake straight away in a preheated oven at 220°C/425°F/Gas 7 for about 8 minutes. For a thicker base, roll out to smaller, thicker circles, put on a baking tray and add the topping. Cover loosely with cling film and leave in a warm place to prove for 10 minutes before baking.

Makes about 700g/1lb 9oz
Preparation time: 15 minutes, plus 1 hour rising
Cooking time: 10 minutes

500g/1lb 2oz/4 cups strong white bread flour, plus extra for dusting
2 tsp salt
10g/¼oz fresh yeast or 5g/⅛oz dried yeast
a little oil, for greasing

Rough puff pastry

Mix together the flour and salt in a bowl, then make a well in the centre and add the butter. Rub in the butter, using your fingertips, until the butter is broken up but still visible in lumps.

Gradually add the cold water, a drop at a time, to bind the ingredients together, but don't overwork the dough as you still want to be able to see the lumps of butter. Wrap in cling film and chill in the fridge for 20–30 minutes.

Roll out the pastry on a lightly floured work surface into a rectangle about 40 x 20cm/16 x 8in with the long side facing you. Fold over one-third of the pastry from each side to make a 13 x 20cm/5 x 8in rectangle, then give it a quarter turn. Repeat this three times, then wrap and chill again for 30 minutes. (If the pastry gets too warm, chill in the fridge for 30 minutes before finishing the folds.)

Makes about 500g/1lb 2oz
Preparation time: 30 minutes,
  plus 1½ hours chilling

250g/9oz/2 cups plain flour,
  plus extra for dusting
1 tsp salt
250g/9oz very cold unsalted butter, diced
125ml/4fl oz/½ cup cold water

Shortcrust pastry

Put the flour in a large bowl, then rub in the butter, using your fingertips, until the mixture resembles coarse breadcrumbs.

Make a well in the centre and add the egg, then bring the mixture together with your hands, adding 1–2 tablespoons water, if necessary, to bind the mixture into a dough.

Turn out onto a cold, lightly floured work surface and knead gently until fully mixed. Wrap in cling film and chill in the fridge for at least 10 minutes before using.

Makes 250g/9oz
Preparation time: 10 minutes,
  plus at least 10 minutes chilling

250g/9oz/2 cups plain flour, plus extra
  for dusting
125g/4½oz cold unsalted butter, diced
1 egg

Anchovy straws

Preheat the oven to 180°C/350°F/Gas 4 and line a baking tray with baking paper.

Lay the pastry on a lightly floured work surface and cut into 1cm/½in strips, then spread the anchovy paste over the pastry. Holding each end of one strip, slowly twist it all the way along, then put it on the prepared baking tray. Repeat with the remaining pastry strips.

Bake for 8–10 minutes until golden brown. Serve warm or cold.

Serves 4
Preparation time: 10 minutes
Cooking time: 10 minutes

250g/9oz ready-rolled all-butter puff pastry
a little flour, for dusting
2 tbsp anchovy paste

Smoked paprika wraps

Mix together the flour, smoked paprika , salt, pepper and baking powder in a bowl. Add the butter and rub together until the mixture resembles breadcrumbs. Gradually add 400ml/14fl oz/generous 1½ cups boiling water, mixing with a wooden spoon and gradually bringing the ingredients together to form a soft dough.

Knead the dough on a lightly floured work surface for 1–2 minutes until smooth, then put in an oiled bowl, cover with cling film and leave for 10 minutes. Divide the dough into 12 equal portions, roll into balls and keep covered.

Put a piece of baking paper on the work surface and dust with flour. Put the first portion of dough on the paper, sprinkle with flour and lay another piece on top. Roll out the dough thinly between the sheets, turning every roll to keep an even shape. Repeat with the rest of the dough.

Heat a large, dry frying pan over a high heat. Add the first wrap and cook for about 30 seconds on each side until just browned. Remove from the pan and leave to cool.

Use straight away or store in an airtight container in the fridge for up to 2 days or freeze for up to a month.

Serves 4
Preparation time: 20 minutes, plus 1 hour rising
Cooking time: 12 minutes

400g/14oz/scant 3¼ cups plain flour, plus extra for dusting
1 tbsp smoked paprika
1 tsp salt
1 tsp freshly ground black pepper
1 tsp baking powder
30g/1oz unsalted butter, diced
a little oil, for greasing

accompaniments

Spiced rice & lentils

Soak the lentils in cold water for 1 hour, then drain well.

Heat the oil and butter in a large saucepan. Add the onion and fry for 1 minute, stirring. Add all the spices and fry for a further 2 minutes.

Drain the lentils, then add them to the pan and cook, stirring, for a further 2 minutes. Add the stock and coriander, season with salt and pepper and bring to the boil. Turn the heat down to low, cover with a lid and simmer for 10 minutes.

Remove from the heat and leave to stand, covered, for 5 minutes, then stir well before serving.

Serves 4
Preparation time: 10 minutes, plus 1 hour soaking, and making the stock
Cooking time: 25 minutes

125g/4.1/2oz/1/2 cup red split lentils
2 tbsp vegetable oil
50g/1 3/4oz unsalted butter
1 onion, finely sliced
1 cinnamon stick
2 cardamom pods
2 cloves
1 red chilli
1 tbsp cumin seeds
1 tsp ground turmeric
500ml/17fl oz/2 cups Vegetable Stock (see page 197)
5 tbsp finely chopped coriander leaves
225g/8oz/scant 1 1/4 cups basmati rice
sea salt and freshly ground black pepper

Saffron rice

Heat the oil and butter in a large saucepan over a medium-high heat. Add the cardamom pods, cinnamon sticks and cumin seeds and fry for 30 seconds.

Add the rice and stir until coated in the butter and oil, then stir in the saffron. Add 1l/35fl oz/4 cups water and the salt and bring to the boil. Turn the heat down to low, cover with a lid and simmer gently for 8–10 minutes until the rice is tender and the water has been absorbed.

Stir through the lemon zest and serve.

Serves 4
Preparation time: 5 minutes
Cooking time: 15 minutes

2 tbsp olive oil
2 tbsp unsalted butter
4 cardamom pods
2 cinnamon sticks
1 tsp cumin seeds
600g/1lb 5oz/3 cups basmati rice, rinsed
a large pinch of saffron strands
1/2 tsp sea salt
grated zest of 2 lemons

Mediterranean vegetable couscous

Put the couscous in a large, heavy-based saucepan over a medium heat and cook for about 5 minutes, shaking the pan frequently and stirring to keep the grains moving around the pan, until the couscous is a lovely mottled, toasted colour. Immediately remove from the heat and tip into a bowl. If you leave it in the pan, it can burn very quickly.

Bring the stock to the boil in a large saucepan over a high heat. Pour over the couscous and stir well. Cover with cling film and leave for 10–15 minutes until the couscous is tender and has absorbed most of the liquid, stirring occasionally. Drain off any excess liquid.

Put the peppers and courgette in a bowl, drizzle with the oil and toss together, then add them to the couscous with the herbs, lemon zest and juice. Season with salt and pepper to taste, then mix together to serve.

Serves 4
Preparation time: 10 minutes, plus
  20 minutes standing, and making the
  stock
Cooking time: 10 minutes

200g/7oz/heaped 1 cup couscous
300ml/10½fl oz/scant 1¼ cups Vegetable
  Stock (see page 197)
1 red pepper, deseeded and finely diced
1 yellow pepper, deseeded and finely diced
1 courgette, finely chopped
2 tbsp olive oil
2 tbsp chopped parsley leaves
1 tbsp chopped mint leaves
grated zest and juice of ½ lemon
sea salt and freshly ground black pepper

Ratatouille

Heat the oil in a large saucepan over a medium heat. Add all the vegetables and the thyme and cook for about 2 minutes.

Add the stock, tomatoes and tomato purée, bring to the boil, then turn the heat down to low and simmer for about 10 minutes. Stir in the pesto and season with a little salt and pepper to taste.

Serve straight away or store in the fridge for up to 3 days and reheat in a saucepan when required.

Serves 4
Preparation time: 20 minutes,
  plus making the stock and pesto
Cooking time: 30 minutes

2 tbsp olive oil
1 onion, finely diced
1 red pepper, deseeded and diced
1 yellow pepper, deseeded and diced
½ aubergine, cut into 1–2cm/½–¾in dice
1 courgette, cut into 1–2cm/½–¾in dice
1 tsp thyme leaves
300ml/10½fl oz/scant 1¼ cups Vegetable
  Stock (see page 197)
250g/9oz/scant 1⅔ cups tinned chopped
  tomatoes
1 tbsp tomato purée
1 tbsp Fresh Basil Pesto (see page 201)
sea salt and freshly ground black pepper

Creamy mashed potatoes

Bring a large saucepan of lightly salted water to the boil over a high heat, add the potatoes and boil for 15–20 minutes until tender, then drain well and return to the pan. Cover and leave to one side to dry for 5 minutes, then mash with a potato masher or put the potato through a potato ricer.

Put the cream, butter and thyme in a small saucepan over a medium heat and bring to the boil. Remove from the heat, discard the thyme and pour the cream into the mash. Season with salt and pepper and bind together with a wooden spoon until well blended. Serve immediately or cool, cover and keep in the fridge for up to 3 days.

Serves 4
Preparation time: 10 minutes
Cooking time: 25 minutes

500g/1lb 2oz floury potatoes, peeled and diced
250ml/9fl oz/1 cup double cream
50g/1¾oz unsalted butter
1 thyme sprig
sea salt and freshly ground black pepper

Roast potatoes

Put the potatoes in a saucepan and rinse under cold water until the water runs completely clear. This will remove much of the starch from the potatoes. Drain, then fill the pan with cold water to cover the potatoes. Bring to the boil over a high heat, then turn the heat down to medium and simmer for about 5–10 minutes until the potatoes are just tender in the centre but not fully cooked.

Drain into a colander, then shake the colander to roughen the edges of the potatoes. Leave them to air dry for at least 5 minutes. Cover and chill in the fridge for at least 1 hour or overnight.

Preheat the oven to 180°C/350°F/Gas 4. Heat the oil and fat in a large roasting tin, then carefully add the potatoes one at a time. Cook on the hob for about 5 minutes, turning with a set of tongs until browned on all sides. Add the thyme and garlic, transfer to the oven and roast for 25 minutes. Turn and move the potatoes around, then return them to the oven for a further 20 minutes until golden and crisp. Drain well before serving.

Serves 4
Preparation time: 10 minutes, plus at least 1 hour drying and chilling
Cooking time: 1 hour

1kg/2lb 4oz good-quality roasting potatoes, such as Maris Piper, King Edward or similar, peeled and cut into even-sized 5cm/2in pieces
200ml/7fl oz/scant 1 cup olive oil
100g/3½oz duck or goose fat
2 thyme sprigs
2 garlic cloves, crushed

Chips

Put the chips in a colander, and the colander in a bowl of cold water and leave to stand for 10 minutes. Rinse in cold water until the water runs clear to remove the starch and help the chips stay crisp. Leave in cold, fresh water.

Heat a deep, heavy-based pan of oil to 150°C/300°F, when a cube of day-old bread browns in 80 seconds. Line a baking tray with kitchen paper. Drain the chips and pat dry on a clean tea towel to remove any water. Gently lower about one-quarter of the chips into the hot oil, so the pan is not too full, and cook for 2–3 minutes until they are soft in the centre if you pinch them. Lift out of the oil using a slotted spoon and transfer to the prepared baking tray. Cook the remaining chips in the same way, then put in the fridge, uncovered, for 10 minutes to chill.

To finish the chips, increase the oil temperature to 180°C/350°F, or when a cube of bread browns in 60 seconds. Add the chips in batches and fry for about 2 minutes until golden and crisp. Remove from the oil, shake dry, then season with a little salt.

Serves 4
Preparation time: 20 minutes, plus 20 minutes standing and chilling
Cooking time: 20 minutes

4 large floury potatoes, such as Maris Piper, peeled and cut into even-sized 1.5cm/⅝in chips
groundnut oil, for deep-frying
sea salt

Potato Dauphinoise

Preheat the oven to 180°C/350°F/Gas 4 and butter a small ovenproof dish. Peel the potatoes, then cut them into 5mm/1¼in slices using a mandolin. Put in a bowl and cover with cold water to prevent them from discolouring. Warm the cream, onion, garlic and thyme in a small saucepan.

Drain the potato slices and start to layer them in the base of the prepared dish, overlapping the edge of the potatoes, seasoning every couple of layers with salt and pepper. Continue until the dish is three-quarters full.

Slowly pour over the garlic and thyme cream, letting it drain through the potato. Sprinkle over the grated cheese and bake in the oven for 20–30 minutes until golden in colour and the potatoes are tender.

Serves 4
Preparation time: 15 minutes
Cooking time: 35 minutes

a little butter, for greasing
500g/1lb 2oz floury potatoes, such as Maris Piper or King Edward
250ml/9fl oz/1 cup double cream
½ onion, finely sliced
1 garlic clove, finely diced
1 tsp chopped thyme leaves
30g/1oz mature Cheddar cheese, grated
sea salt and freshly ground black pepper

Potato croquettes

Preheat the oven to 160°C/315°F/Gas 2½. Put the cold mashed potatoes in a bowl. If you like, mix in your chosen flavouring to taste. Put the breadcrumbs in a shallow bowl. Whisk together the eggs and milk in another shallow bowl with a pinch of salt to make an egg wash.

Heat 4cm/1½in of oil in a frying pan to 180°C/350°F, when a cube of bread browns in 50 seconds.

Take a tablespoonful of the mash at a time and roll into a ball. Dip the potato balls in the egg wash, shake off any excess, then roll in the breadcrumbs.

Add the croquettes to the hot oil a few at a time and fry for about 3 minutes until heated through and browned on all sides. Lift out of the pan, using a slotted spoon, drain on kitchen paper, then put in the oven to keep warm until you have fried the remaining croquettes.

Serves 4
Preparation time: 20 minutes,
  plus making the mash
Cooking time: 15 minutes

1 recipe quantity Creamy Mashed Potatoes
  (see page 212), chilled
flavourings, such as cooked smoked
  bacon, mustard, 1 tbsp chopped chives,
  tarragon or other herb (optional)
100g/3½oz/1 cup panko breadcrumbs
2 eggs
2 tbsp milk
olive oil, for frying
sea salt and freshly ground black pepper

Parmentier potatoes

Trim the sides of the potatoes to make them square, then cut into 1cm/½in slices. Cut the slices into 1cm/½in strips, then the strips into 1cm/½in cubes. Rinse under cold water to remove the excess starch.

Heat the groundnut oil in a deep, heavy-based saucepan to 170°C/325°F, when a cube of bread will brown in 60 seconds. Add the potatoes and fry for about 5 minutes until golden. Drain on kitchen paper, season well with salt and pepper and serve.

Serves 4
Preparation time: 10 minutes
Cooking time: 10 minutes

600g/1lb 5oz floury potatoes, such as
  King Edward or Maris Piper, peeled
groundnut oil, for deep-frying
sea salt and freshly ground black pepper

Sweet potato wedges

Preheat the oven to 200°C/400°F/Gas 6.

Put the sweet potato wedges in a baking tray, skin-side down, drizzle with the oil, sprinkle with the smoked paprika and season with a little salt and pepper. Bake for 20–30 minutes until crisp on the outside and slightly soft in the centre. Serve hot.

Serves 4
Preparation time: 4 minutes
Cooking time: 30 minutes

4 sweet potatoes, cut into wedges
  lengthways
3 tbsp olive oil
½ tsp smoked paprika
sea salt and freshly ground black pepper

Sweet potato or parsnip crisps

Using a vegetable peeler, cut thin strips off the sweet potatoes or parsnips, from top to bottom, while turning the vegetable so you are peeling it evenly into long strips.

Heat the oil in a deep, heavy-based saucepan to 160°C/315°F, when a cube of bread browns in 70 seconds. Using a slotted spoon, gently lower a spoonful of the vegetable strips into the hot oil and cook for 2–3 minutes, gently turning them in the oil until they are evenly golden in colour. Lift out of the pan, using a slotted spoon, and drain on kitchen paper. Continue to fry the remaining vegetables. Season with salt and pepper to taste.

Serve sprinkled on any chicken dish or just as a tasty snack.

Serves 4
Preparation time: 10 minutes
Cooking time: 10 minutes

2 sweet potatoes or 4 parsnips, peeled
400ml/14fl oz/generous 1½ cups
  groundnut oil
sea salt and freshly ground black pepper

Honey-roasted root vegetables

Preheat the oven to 200°C/400°F/Gas 6. Bring a saucepan of water to the boil over a high heat, add the parsnips, carrots and celeriac and boil for 4 minutes until just soft in the middle. Drain and refresh under cold water to stop them cooking further, then drain again. Put in a roasting tray and season with salt and pepper.

Whisk together the honey and mustard, then drizzle over the vegetables and roast for 15–20 minutes until golden in colour, shaking halfway through to coat the vegetables in the honey and mustard.

Serves 4
Preparation time: 15 minutes
Cooking time: 30 minutes

200g/7oz parsnips, cut into batons
200g/7oz carrots, cut into batons
200g/7oz celeriac, cut into batons
2 tbsp clear honey
1 tbsp Dijon mustard
1 tsp chopped thyme leaves
sea salt and freshly ground black pepper

Buttered carrots

Bring a saucepan of water to the boil over a high heat. Add the carrots and cook for 2 minutes, then run under cold water until cold, or put into a bowl of ice-cold water to stop them cooking further. Drain, then return to the pan.

Add the butter and parsley to the carrots and put the pan over a medium heat. Cook in the pan for 3–4 minutes until the carrots are hot and covered in the herb butter. Serve straight away or cool and reheat when required.

Serves 4
Preparation time: 5 minutes
Cooking time: 10 minutes

400g/14oz Chantenay carrots,
   halved lengthways
1 tbsp unsalted butter
2 tbsp chopped parsley leaves

Golden onions

Heat the oil in a saucepan over a medium heat. Add the onions and fry quickly for 1–2 minutes until light golden in colour.

Add enough water to come halfway up the onions and stir in the sugar. Heat, stirring, until the sugar has melted, then bring to the boil. Turn the heat down to low and simmer for about 15 minutes until the onions are just tender and the liquid has reduced to a syrup.

Serves 4
Preparation time: 5 minutes
Cooking time: 20 minutes

3 tbsp olive oil
250g/9oz baby onions, peeled
50g/1¾oz/¼ cup caster sugar

Wilted greens

Bring a saucepan of water to the boil over a high heat. Add the cabbage and cook for 2 minutes, then drain and put into a bowl of ice-cold water to stop it from cooking further. Drain well.

Melt the butter in a saucepan over a medium heat. Add the drained cabbage and stir for 1–2 minutes, then add the spinach and stir for 3–4 minutes until the spinach has softened and is warm. Season with a little salt and pepper to taste. Serve straight from the pan.

Serves 4
Preparation time: 5 minutes
Cooking time: 10 minutes

½ Savoy cabbage, finely sliced
2 tbsp unsalted butter
250g/9oz spinach leaves
sea salt and freshly ground black pepper

Celeriac rémoulade

Mix together the celeriac and lemon juice in a non-metallic bowl. Stir in all the remaining ingredients and season with salt and pepper to taste. Serve straight from the bowl.

Serves 4
Preparation time: 10 minutes,
    plus making the mayonnaise

400g/14oz celeriac, peeled and grated
    into long strips
juice of ½ lemon
5 tbsp Mayonnaise (see page 202)
3 tbsp drained capers, finely chopped
2 tbsp chopped parsley leaves
1 tbsp chopped chives
1 tbsp double cream

Slow-roasted tomatoes

Preheat the oven to the lowest possible heat, 100°C/200°F/ Gas 1. Slice the tomatoes straight down the centre, then cut each half into wedges, making sure all the wedges are the same size. Put on a baking tray, skin-side down. Drizzle with a little of the olive oil, then sprinkle with the salt, garlic and thyme leaves.

Roast for 4–6 hours until dried but still slightly flexible, checking every hour as you don't want them to dry completely. Leave to cool.

Spoon into a screw-topped jar and cover with the remaining oil. Store in the fridge for up to a month.

Makes about 400g/14oz
Preparation time: 10 minutes
Cooking time: 6 hours

12 large vine tomatoes
50–100ml/1½–3½fl oz/3 tbsp–scant ½ cup olive oil
2 tbsp sea salt crystals
3 garlic cloves, roughly chopped
leaves from 3 thyme sprigs

Celeriac & carrot coleslaw

Put the celeriac, carrot and onion in a bowl and toss together.

Mix the mayonnaise with the mustard and lemon juice and season with salt and pepper to taste. Serve at once, or transfer to an airtight container and keep in the fridge for up to 3 days.

Serves 4
Preparation time: 15 minutes, plus making the mayonnaise

100g/3½oz celeriac, peeled and finely grated
100g/3½oz carrot, peeled and finely grated
50g/1¾oz onion, finely sliced
3–4 tbsp Mayonnaise (see page 202)
2 tsp Dijon mustard (optional)
1 tsp lemon juice
sea salt and freshly ground black pepper

Green salad

Put all the ingredients in a bowl, then drizzle over the salad dressing, season with salt and pepper and toss gently to combine. Serve immediately.

Serves 4
Preparation time: 10 minutes

4 spring onions, diagonally sliced
2 Little Gem lettuce, finely sliced
½ cucumber, sliced lengthways then cut
   into thin strips
100g/3½oz baby spinach leaves, chopped
50g/1¾oz mangetout, finely sliced
1 tbsp Bean House Salad Dressing
   (see page 203)

Herb salad

Put all the herbs in a bowl, sprinkle over the sesame seeds, then drizzle over the salad dressing and toss gently to combine. Serve immediately.

Serves 4
Preparation time: 10 minutes

50g/1¾oz flat-leaf parsley leaves, chopped
50g/1¾oz coriander leaves, roughly chopped
2 tbsp chopped chives
60g/2¼oz rocket leaves or watercress leaves
40g/1½oz mint leaves, roughly chopped
20g/¾oz basil leaves, roughly torn
3 tbsp toasted sesame seeds
1–2 tbsp Bean House Salad Dressing
   (see page 203)

Microleaf & carrot salad

Put all the ingredients together in a bowl, then drizzle the dressing over the salad and toss together gently. Serve immediately.

Serves 4
Preparation time: 10 minutes

50g/1¾oz tenderstem pea shoots
50g/1¾oz borage leaves
50g/1¾oz garlic chives, chopped
60g/2¼oz micro watercress
40g/1½oz micro coriander
50g/1¾oz micro red vein sorrel
30g/1oz finely grated carrot
1–2 tbsp Bean House Salad Dressing
   (see page 203)

index

acknowledgements

A big thanks to Grace Cheetham for asking me to write this book. I have to admit it was a lot harder than I first thought, but I got there in the end. Thanks, Grace, Rebecca, Wendy and the team, for bearing with me.

An enormous vote of thanks has to go to my wife, Jenny, and our daughters, Ella and Ava, for supporting me while I've been working all day and through the night testing recipes and typing.

A big thank you to my butcher – John Sykes from Shrewsbury market – for supplying me with lots of chicken.

Thanks to Dave Parker, a good friend and top chef, for helping me develop and test some of the recipes.

I hope everyone likes it and that in some way it helps you all on your own culinary journey.

NOURISH

EAT WELL, LIVE WELL

We hope you've enjoyed this Nourish book. Here at Nourish we're all about wellbeing through food and drink – irresistible dishes with a serious good-for-you factor. If you want to eat and drink delicious things that set you up for the day, suit any special diets, keep you healthy and make the most of what you can afford, we've got some great ideas to share with you. Come over to our blog for wholesome recipes and fresh inspiration – nourishbooks.com.